CONFIDENT
POWERBOATING

CONFIDENT
POWERBOATING

Mastering Skills and
Avoiding Trouble Afloat

Stuart Reininger

INTERNATIONAL MARINE / McGRAW-HILL

Camden, Maine ❑ New York ❑ Chicago ❑ San Francisco ❑ Lisbon ❑ London ❑ Madrid
Mexico City ❑ Milan ❑ New Delhi ❑ San Juan ❑ Seoul ❑ Singapore ❑ Sydney ❑ Toronto

The **McGraw·Hill** Companies

2 3 4 5 6 7 8 9   DOC DOC   0 9 8

Library of Congress Cataloging-in-Publication Data
Reininger, Stuart.
    Confident powerboating : mastering skills and avoiding trouble afloat / Stuart Reininger.
        p.   cm.
    Includes index.
    ISBN 978-0-07-148257-8 (pbk. : alk. paper)
    1. Motorboats.   2. Boats and boating.   I. Title.
    GV835.R45 2008
    797.12'5—dc22   2008001945

ISBN 978-0-07-148257-8
MHID 0-07-148257-1

www.internationalmarine.com

Questions regarding the ordering of this book should be addressed to
The McGraw-Hill Companies
Customer Service Department
P.O. Box 547
Blacklick, OH 43004
Retail customers: 1-800-262-4729
Bookstores: 1-800-722-4726

Photographs by author unless otherwise noted.
Title page photo by Steve D'Antonio.
Illustrations by Christopher Hoyt.

Contents

Acknowledgments

MANY PEOPLE HELPED in the creation of this book. I would especially like to thank Capt. Skip Shepherd for sharing his extraordinary boat-handling skills and marine knowledge; Rosalie Shepherd for her line-handling and modeling expertise; Dan Bair of Quality Boats of Clearwater, Florida, for the use of his facilities; John Malenda for his technical and artistic expertise; Capt. Joe McGuinness and the crew of Sea Tow of Eastern Connecticut for contributing their time and vessels; Ed Milley for his technical advice and mechanical skills; James Mitchell III of Noank, Connecticut, for his thoughts on modern fiberglass powerboat management; Hollyce Yoken for her insightful comments on the manuscript; Jorulf Tranoy for his explanation of Norwegian boating techniques and his assistance with the art program; the Regal Boat Corporation for supplying vessels; the Winslow Life Raft Company for sharing its photo archives and, incidentally, for building the raft that saved my life; Ft. Rachel Marina, Mystic, Connecticut, for allowing the use of their facilities and staff; Steve and Geoff Jones of the West Mystic Wooden Boat Yard for their support and advice; the staff of the Mystic & Noank Library for recognizing that I wasn't really a vagrant; and last, but far from least, Bob Holtzman, my McGraw-Hill editor, for his patience and sense of humor, which undoubtedly contributed toward maintaining his sanity while working with me.

Introduction

AMONG THE TRUTHS ABOUT boating and flying is that there are plenty of pilots who are boaters and vice versa. One reason is that both groups are devotees of procedure—time-tested methods and systems that work. We have our checklists, walk-around inspections, and dedicated niches for tools and gear so that they can be accessed when needed. We share orderly minds and a wary respect for the seas and skies personified by the credo that there are bold boaters/pilots and old boaters/pilots, but there are no old, bold boaters/pilots.

We also need to react quickly to rapidly changing circumstances: the sudden storm, the unpredictable equipment failure, and the looming catastrophe. Sometimes, all our planning and preparation go out the window; an unexpected situation occurs, and our carefully considered Plans B and C are suddenly useless. Then we may have to think out of the box and maybe jury-rig a solution.

That's where we boaters enjoy a certain advantage over our aviator friends. We've been sailing the seas, reacting to the unexpected, and jury-rigging since before Icarus cast questioning eyes aloft. Embedded in long-established nautical tradition is the understanding that in spite of a respect for the orderly and methodical approach, boaters have to be prepared to be totally unorthodox—we need to know when to break the rules. And that's part of what this book is about.

Somewhat more than thirty years ago, I began a career on the water working alongside charter and delivery skippers whose goals were to move boats quickly and efficiently. We worked with the knowledge that if we got in trouble, no one was going to bail us out. Most of us were in no position to turn down a job, so we traveled long distances aboard boats that wouldn't be allowed off a dock today and too often experienced the kind of mishaps that proof-tested the efficacy of various responses. Assuming we survived both physically and professionally (we usually did), those responses, whether successful or not, added to our stock of experience and helped guide future responses to similar incidents.

With modern boats, up-to-date equipment, and today's support systems (ranging from commercial towing services to GPS, whose simplicity and accuracy were unimaginable just a few years ago), many of those procedures and methods have been all but forgotten. But navigable waters are still the same contrary beasts they always were. Things continue to go wrong, and help isn't always available. So in this book are tried and true procedures from decades of experience that you'll find useful in situations that are routine but difficult as well as in situations where things go wrong or the unexpected occurs. Some of the techniques are unconventional but are just the ticket for dealing with those unexpected and unwelcome surprises that *will* occur when you spend enough time on the water.

This book doesn't attempt to teach basic seamanship skills. It's assumed that you can handle maneuvers like approaching and leaving a dock alongside when the wind and current are cooperating; that, given good visibility and reasonable sea conditions, you can steer a straight course and negotiate a marked channel without transferring paint from any aids to navigation to your topsides; and that you know what to do in straightforward crossing and overtaking situations with other boats. (If any of these things are beyond your skill level at the moment, there are plenty of excellent books to get you up to speed. You'll find several listed in the Appendix.)

But there's a world of difference between a boater with beginner-level skills and a *confident* powerboater with intermediate-level skills. Some boaters never move beyond the beginner stage. They either confine themselves to boating in ideal conditions as much as possible, thus greatly restricting their time on the water and limiting their enjoyment of boating, or they attempt to push their limits without having the necessary knowledge. Many who push their limits experience enough problems and make enough mistakes to get themselves into big trouble, which turns them back into a "fair weather only" boater or turns them off of boating altogether.

The goal of this book is to turn you from a boater with beginner-level skills into a confident, intermediate-level boater, by showing you how to handle situations that are a bit, or a lot, trickier. You'll learn how to dock under adverse conditions as well as how to handle bad weather, challenging sea conditions, and rough inlets. Since many powerboaters have poor anchoring skills or avoid anchoring altogether, anchoring "basics" will be treated as an intermediate-level skill. More advanced anchoring techniques will be addressed as well—the ones you'll need when the situation is more difficult. You'll learn how to handle larger problems, such as when the engine dies, something important breaks, or you or another boater needs a tow. Finally, handling true emergency situations, such as fires, flooding, grounding, and sinking, will be covered. Assuming that none of us wants to learn these latter sets of skills through experience, I've made *Confident Powerboating* the next best thing, to give you the information you need to handle events that range from inconvenient to life-threatening with confidence.

Along the way, you'll read a number of stories about boaters who overcame serious problems, and some who, well, blew it. And I'll admit to making mistakes myself a few times. I appear in a magazine ad for a leading life raft manufacturer, and although it's not the kind of publicity that a professional delivery captain normally seeks, I'm glad to provide the endorsement because his excellent product saved my life. While I was sitting in that raft waiting for rescue, I thought about what I had done wrong and what I could have done differently so that I could have avoided becoming a poster child for emergency equipment.

There is nothing discussed in this book that I haven't personally applied or experienced. Hopefully, you'll never encounter some of the situations covered here, but there's all too good a chance that at least some of these scenarios are in your boating future. It is best to be prepared.

1
Docking Made Easy

THERE'S AN OLD SAYING among pilots that flying is easy; the tricky part is getting down again. The parallels between flyers and boaters are obvious. Flyers, however, hold an advantage over us; a great proportion of their required flight instruction is aimed at safe landings. For the most part, boaters receive little formal training, learning our "landings" empirically through trial and error. Of course, the repercussions of a faulty docking attempt are usually a lot less traumatic than a pilot's bad landing. Still, a bad docking procedure can be *really* bad, resulting, at a minimum, in embarrassment and frayed nerves, and potentially involving various levels of property damage and even physical injury.

Since docking is something we have to do nearly every time we go boating, it can be considered an essential skill of seamanship. Doing it poorly can sap your confidence and kill your enjoyment of boating. Doing it effectively, on the other hand, is a great confidence-builder. Once you learn how to make your boat perform the precise, accurate maneuvers that docking requires, you'll be proud to demonstrate your abilities to others, and you'll be more capable of performing other close-quarters maneuvers.

The boats we drive are equipped with a variety of power and drive systems, including inboards, outboards, stern drives (also known as inboard-outboards, or I/Os), and jet drives. And there are single- and twin-engine versions of all of these. (Yes, there are also triples and even quadruples, but from a handling point of view, these are very similar to twins.) But no matter what type of boat you own and for whatever reason you purchased it, you have to dock it, and it won't be long before your particular vessel's idiosyncrasies assert themselves.

There is a long-standing belief that while outboards and stern drives are more maneuverable—primarily by being able to make tighter turns—they are "squirrelly" around the dock, more likely to skid around and react to current and breeze than inboards. Well, yes and no. As a rule, inboard vessels, both singles and twins, tend to be more forgiving, due to the greater depth of their props, the angle of the prop shaft in the water, and the fact that the boat is turned via its rudder. These factors tend to produce a more deliberate or controlled response to an unexpected breeze or current rip. In contrast, outboards and stern drives are more sensitive to changes in shift and throttle due to the generally shallower prop arrangement and the fact that steering is accomplished by changing the direction of the props themselves. By eliminating the middleman of the rudder, steering reaction is more instantaneous.

Is this a good thing? Again, yes and no. Quicker response presents more of a possibility of oversteering, or applying too much power to compensate for wind and current. But it doesn't take long for a savvy operator to recognize this and use it to advantage. It's simply a function of using the boat often enough to become comfortable with it.

One area of knowledge that comes with experience is the proper use of engine or outdrive trim. Most boaters learn sooner or later to adjust the vertical angle of their outboard or stern drive to get onto plane more efficiently, and to improve ride and handling once they're there. But proper engine trim applies to slow-speed maneuvers around docks as well. Unless the water is unusually shallow, the lower units should be trimmed all the way down. This gives them better bite in the water and that more deliberate sense of control that inboard advocates favor—but without giving up anything on the rapid response side of the ledger.

I've found that the newer generation of twin-prop stern drives—Volvo Penta's DuoProp drives and MerCruiser's Bravo III drives—and their advanced and smoother transmissions tend to negate many of the handling differences between inboard and stern-drive power. Improved lower unit and prop technology allow close-in handling comparable to any inboard. The bottom line is that once you become familiar with the boat you're operating, it'll do what you need it to do, no matter what the propulsion system.

While there are obvious advantages to maneuvering with twins, the single-screw operator has a few things going for him or her also. Think prop walk. Props are either right-hand turning or left-hand turning. Most single-screw boats have a right-hand turning prop; check yours to be sure—it's usually marked "RH" or "LH" on the hub, or just watch the prop when it turns. When viewed from astern, if the prop turns clockwise when in forward gear, it's a right-hand prop.

A right-hand prop will turn a boat tighter to starboard when coming ahead, and kick the stern to port in reverse. (Vice versa with a left-hand prop.) That's good to know when maneuvering—especially around the dock. With my single-screw boat, for instance, I love to back into a slip when the boarding ramp is to port, since I know that the boat will kick in that direction. With quick bursts of power in forward or reverse, you can shift the stern sideways without putting on much, if any, way ahead or astern.

In any docking or other close-quarters situation, remember that wind and current rule. No matter what type of boat you're handling and no matter the power, if you're caught unexpectedly broadside to wind and/or current, you'll be surprised how fast and far that leeward set can be—especially when there's something, such as a piling, a dock, or another boat, in the way. Whenever in doubt or caught unaware, and if there's time and room, get the bow or stern into the wind or current, which will allow you to regain control and think things out.

What we don't address here is the ideal situation: pulling up to the dock into the wind or current. That's because it's a no-brainer. Practice it a few times and you'll see why. Just think ahead, *go slow*, and see how your boat reacts when approaching the dock into wind or current. It'll *want* to make a good landing; you're just there to help it along.

Docking. 1. The boat approaches the dock at a relatively sharp angle. The approach is into wind and/or current. 2. At bare steerageway, the skipper is right off the dock preparing to move the helm to port and modify the approach at a shallower angle. 3. The helm is over, and the boat begins to parallel the dock. 4. Alongside, the skipper is ready to deploy mooring lines.

A Lunchtime Lesson

I WAS HAVING LUNCH with my old partner John and a client of his at a dockside Ft. Lauderdale bistro when a snazzy twin-outboard-powered runabout swung around, and the skipper, skillfully compensating for the current, shaped up to back into a slip. All went well until his stern was centered between the pilings, where there was little or no current, with the bow still into the fast-running stream. When the current grabbed the bow and began to corkscrew the boat around, the runabout's skipper compensated by twisting the wheel in the opposite direction and hitting hard reverse. The boat shot astern, and only the skipper's quick reflexes in coming ahead prevented those pretty outboards from slamming into the seawall. But the boat came ahead with gusto also, and by the time the ping-ponging ceased and the boat made fast, its skipper looked like he had already lost his appetite.

"And that's one reason I stay away from outboards," John's client piped up. Now, here's a guy blithely preparing to cruise his 60-foot yacht throughout southern Florida and the Bahamas who is being intimidated by an outboard. John, who makes his living teaching people how to handle their yachts, later mentioned that's not an unusual opinion from people who've been tooling around in inboards and then step into an outboard.

"You handle them very similarly," John said. "But you have to recognize and understand some basic differences—and those differences are most apparent when maneuvering around the dock."

John's absolutely right. First of all, most outboards don't have the deeper "bite" that inboard props have. Therefore, it often takes a little more application of power to accomplish the same result. But that power must be applied gradually. The new driver will apply power in bursts, which in an inboard can be beneficial in kicking a bow or stern around. In an outboard, that burst of power can manifest itself quicker than in an inboard, resulting in the vessel shooting ahead or astern faster than intended. This is particularly true in reverse where most outboards have significantly more torque than in forward.

Many outboards, especially older ones, experience an instant of delay after shifting. If you don't wait until the engine actually kicks in gear and continue advancing the throttle until it does, you'll end up feeding more fuel to the engine than you intend, causing that disconcerting "outboard leap-frogging."

"That initial jump, especially with an older outboard or a stiff shifting arrangement, is what will get you into trouble when maneuvering," John said. "Practice easing the throttle from neutral into forward or reverse past the detent and then feeding as little fuel as possible to the engine."

Boaters going from twin inboards to twin outboards will quickly realize that playing the engines against each other—running one engine in forward with the other in neutral or reverse to spin or turn the boat—isn't nearly as effective with outboards. Generally, outboard props are closer together, thus limiting their effectiveness when working in different gears to twist the boat on its pivot point. On the other hand, since outboard lower units serve as their own rudders, outboard twins working together will turn tighter than inboard twins.

The skipper of this twin-engine outboard is holding its fendered bow against the dock by applying power gently forward and adjusting the helm in response to the boat's motion. She can easily hold the boat against the dock until proper lines are in place.

With no power applied, the boat drifts away from the dock.

With the boat in gentle forward gear, the bow line will tighten and the stern will push out allowing the boat to "spring off" the dock. This maneuver will be facilitated by turning the wheel (and thus the props) toward the dock. The bow should always be fendered.

Another twin-outboard towboat has pulled in for a quick tie-up. The fore-and-aft springs running from his aft starboard cleat are made up of one long line. Note the bow line running from the forward cleat to the dock; that will keep his bow from swinging out. He also has a spring line led forward from a midships cleat to the dock, but that's extraneous as it replicates the spring farther aft.

BASIC BACKING PROCEDURES FOR TWINS

Arguably, backing into a slip is among the most anxiety-producing maneuvers in boating. It doesn't need to be if you keep the following in mind:

- The effects of wind and current are always greater on the bow than the stern.
- The importance of centering the rudders of inboards and the lower units of stern drives and outboards cannot be overemphasized. If the inboard boat is not equipped with rudder position indicators, bring the wheel all the way to the port or starboard stop and then turn in the opposite direction, counting the turns of the wheel to the opposite stop; turn back half the number of turns and the rudder is centered. At that point, under normal backing circumstances, there should be no need to use the rudder. All steering will be with the screws.
- The boat will "twist" in reverse, the same way it will in forward gear except in the opposite direction (more power to the port engine in reverse and the boat will move to the right as it progresses backward and vice versa). The difference is that the bow of the boat—the "stern" as it progresses in reverse—will be more sensitive to wind and current. Overcompensating to correct for that drift is the most common error made while backing.
- While the essential maneuvers are the same, generally outboards and stern drives tend to be a bit more sensitive in this type of maneuvering than inboards. A common error is for the operator to apply too much power and then overcompensate to correct. Power—and shifting—must always be gradual and eased into. (See The Chubby Checker Twins Technique on page 8.) It shouldn't take much practice (try backing between floats or marker buoys in open water) for you to get the hang of your boat's particular characteristics.

Keeping the above points in mind, I've found the following procedure helpful when backing:

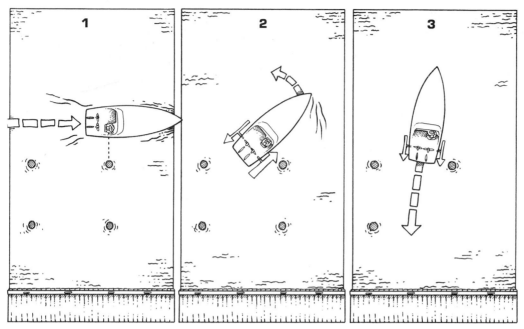

To back into slip: 1. Stop with most of the boat beyond the far piling of the slip and set both rudders or drives amidships. 2. Place the screw on the side opposite the slip in reverse and the screw on the nearside in forward. You may need more throttle on the nearside to counter the greater torque of the reversed screw. 3. Shift the nearside screw into reverse, and back both engines.

1. When proceeding to the intended slip, focus on the farther piling of the two that the boat will be backed between. (See panel 1 of the illustration above.)

2. When that piling is directly across from the operator (assuming a conventional aft-helmed cruiser), bring the boat to a complete stop, center the helm, and begin to line the boat up with the slip.

3. Reverse the engine to get the boat started in the proper direction (port engine if the slip is to starboard). If it's necessary to kick the opposing engine forward to increase the swing, there should be a lag as well as less revs in that direction. The idea is to swing, not continue forward. Having to overcome forward motion when beginning the swing is a common error that often leads to overcompensation. Another common error is beginning to move astern before the boat is properly lined up. The boat then needs to turn and move astern simultaneously, making the procedure more difficult. Also, when there's way on astern, the swing is less predictable and lends itself to overcompensation. The time to move astern is when the boat is lined up between the pilings. (See panel 2.)

4. When compensating for the bow falling off in the opposite direction, remember that torque in reverse is greater than in forward gear. Therefore, when increasing the revs

of one engine in reverse, all things being equal, speed astern will increase and the stern will be kicked in the opposite direction. To allow the boat to compensate for the bow drift without increasing speed astern, forward rpm must be applied to the opposite screw—usually more revs in forward are required than revs astern to compensate for the increased torque of the opposing reversed engine.

4. Then, when you're lined up, put your other engine in reverse to continue a straight course. (See panel 3.)

Nothing is perfect but practice helps.

The Chubby Checker Twins Technique

OKAY, SO YOU'VE FINALLY moved up to the big twin of your dreams, and you know, intellectually, how twin engines maneuver a boat—port engine ahead, starboard neutral or reverse and the boat turns right and vice versa—but it's not *instinctive* yet. There you are in the middle of a tight docking situation and you're tossing shifts and throttles every which way. Suddenly you go blank, and you have to take time to *think* but you just don't have the time and the @#$% boat goes the wrong way.

Well, that was me back in the days of wooden boats and iron heads when my old single-screw Elco threw its last plank and I moved up to a somewhat less ancient twin-engine Chris Craft Connie. I always forgot which handle to push when things started getting dicey—until Chubby Checker came along and taught me the "Twist." It wasn't the real Chubby, of course; it was an old delivery skipper I was crewing for who didn't need any more gray hairs from a clueless kid. Use body English, he said, do the "Twist." Put your hands on the shifts, put them in neutral, and face forward. Need to go to starboard? Twist your body to the right; the left hand moves forward—shift ahead, right hand/shift moves backward, astern; boat twists to starboard. Going to port? Twist to the left—left

Doing the "Twist" is an effective way to get the hang of selecting the right shift directions when backing.

shift goes astern, right shift moves forward/ahead, and boat moves to port.

The same method works going astern. For instance, assuming both shifts are in neutral, if you need to move to starboard while backing, twist your left shoulder back and your right shoulder forward. With your left hand on the gearshift lever, it'll naturally shift into reverse. Of course, not all turns need the opposing thrust of the other engine, and it'll be up to you, depending on the circumstances, to decide whether your other hand will shift the other engine into forward or just caress the handle.

BACKING INBOARD AND STERN-DRIVE SINGLES

With single-screw boats, backing is a whole different game. This is where spring lines and efficient fendering can save the day. Often, especially when the boat is a light, small stern drive and the wind and/or current are piping, it's better to lie alongside the piling(s) and spring the stern around than to back in. The procedure is as follows:

1. Secure a line to an aft cleat, run the working end around a piling, and loop the line with plenty of tail around the same cleat. (See photo 1 below.)
2. Have the crew ease the line out as the boat is backed down. (See photo 3 on the following page.)
3. When the stern is projecting well between the pilings, have the crew secure the line and carefully apply reverse power. (See photo 5.)
4. As the stern springs around, ease the line for more control. When the boat is lined up properly, the spring line is eased and the boat moves astern into the slip.

Using a spring line to back into a slip.
1. This single-screw cruiser is preparing to spring astern into the slip. The skipper has maneuvered alongside the piling, the crew has looped a line around the piling and is now easing the line as the skipper prepares to reverse.

2. The crew takes the slack out of the line at the skipper's command as he begins to swing around the piling and into the slip.

(continued)

(continued)

3. The captain cuts the wheel to port and comes gently astern. The crew is able to apply tension on the line by holding it in her hands as the weather is relatively calm. If the wind were blowing harder, she would take a turn around the port aft cleat and ease the line as the boat comes astern. 4. The boat swings around the piling utilizing the leverage of the spring line. Note the fender between the piling and vessel. 5. The boat is lined up between the pilings. The helm is centered as the skipper backs in; the crew eases the line as the boat goes astern. 6. He's alongside the dock now and preparing to move back the last few feet and tie off. 7. The crew ties the fore-and-aft springs in place as the skipper ducks below for a well-earned libation.

Proper fendering when backing is important as the boat will be pivoting on the piling. That's when a fenderboard comes in handy. For some reason, these handy devices are going out of style and are seen on fewer boats. Fenderboards don't take much space—they can be as simple as mahogany two-by-twos with bronze ¾-inch half-round strips running along the side that will be facing the dock. When slung over a couple of fenders, you'll avoid contact between the hull and piling.

This fenderboard has been put to good use. Note that the fenders are near the ends of the board to prevent the board from pivoting on the fenders and contacting the hull.

DOWNWIND AND DOWNCURRENT DOCKING

I knew problems were afoot when we lost an engine and at the same time I spotted a whiff of smoke drifting out of the engine compartment. But I wasn't quick enough to stop one of the passengers from immediately yanking the engine hatch off to see what was up. Within seconds flames boiled out of the compartment—which was surrounded by a half-dozen people either immobilized by shock or contemplating a dive overboard. They were all one family, and I had been hired by their patriarch to familiarize him in the operation of their brand-new 45-foot express cruiser.

I had just begun to shape up for a landing on New Jersey's Maurice River—a dredged current-ridden cut that empties into Delaware Bay. That option faded as it was a fuel dock, and I was planning to put the cruiser between two refueling fishing boats. However, immediately downstream was an unoccupied work dock. Fortunately, our lines were already prepared; without bothering to turn into the current, I aimed for that dock. I grabbed a teenage scion and told him that I would put the bow against the nearest piling and instructed him to grab the line that I had secured to the bow cleat earlier and to step on the dock and take a couple turns of the line around a piling. He did just that, and with that line acting as a fulcrum, the fast-moving current swiveled the boat around and slammed it alongside the dock—bow facing upstream.

Within seconds, everybody was safely off and the boat's fire suppression system and a manual extinguisher put the fire out. Damage was surprisingly minimal, just burnt wiring and insulation in the engine room (a belt had thrown and the alarm hadn't gone off) and scratched gelcoat where the hull slammed into the pilings.

Fast thinking on my part? Sure, but my actions weren't off the cuff. I followed a pre-planned procedure for just such a situation. Nobody wants to dock downwind/-current, but we all need to be prepared for the eventuality—but, hopefully, not under similar circumstances.

Under ideal conditions—wind and current on the bow and a long unoccupied dock alongside—a single- or twin-screw boat will just about berth itself. Just think where you want to lay it, and with a little throttle action and a touch of the helm, it's alongside. Having the wind or current on the bow allows you to play the boat's forward momentum, and forward power, against the natural forces, and steering in forward is absolutely easier. A little more power, and you move ahead; a little less, and you shift astern; in between, and you stay where you are. You can even do what canoeists call a "ferry"—come parallel to the dock exactly opposite of where you want to berth. Put the engines ahead at exactly the same speed that the wind or current is pushing you astern so that you go neither ahead nor astern. Steer just a hair toward the dock, and the boat will shift sideways and sidle right up where you want it.

Unfortunately, we sometimes have to dock downcurrent or downwind. Such an approach is never preferable because then you have to counter the natural force with the engine(s) in reverse and no boat steers as well in reverse as it does in forward. Situations occur, however, where an emergency exists and a traditional docking is not an option. I have had to dock downwind on various occasions, including once with a seriously overheated engine where, if I had taken the time to shape up properly, it would have seized. Other occasions included an approach to a dock in a crowded, narrow fairway where there wasn't room to turn around due to heavy traffic behind me, as well as that time of a raging engine fire when I needed to get people off immediately. If there's no possible way to get headed upstream, the next two sections outline the procedures that work for me for twin and single screws. As with other procedures that don't involve grave danger, they should be practiced—preferably when conditions are benign.

Twin Screws

When docking a twin screw downwind or downcurrent, I use this procedure:

1. Fenders are placed on the dockside of the boat. A nylon dockline is secured to the dockside midships cleat. Bow and stern lines are bent to their respective cleats, positioned, and secured so they will not inadvertently fall overboard. (See photo 1 below.)

2. The boat is placed close to and parallel to the dock. In the following wind/current, the stern will tend to kick out at an angle to the dock. This is best compensated for by placing the opposite-dock engine in reverse. When the dockside cleat is directly opposite the midships cleat, the looped end of the midships docking line is passed to the person on the dock with instructions to place the loop on the cleat. (See photo 5.)

3. The crew is instructed to take up on the midships cleat line as soon as possible. The less distance between the dock cleat and the midships cleat, the easier the landing will be as the stern will tend to swing out and place the (fendered) bow against the dock. (See photo 6.)

4. As soon as the boat is stationary, bow and stern lines are secured and the midships line released and led aft to a cleat on the dock to become a spring line. A forward spring is also prepared.

5. In the event the boat is not equipped with a midships cleat or a dock attendant is not available, the procedure can be performed as a single-screw downwind berthing.

Docking with twin screws. 1. This twin-screw cruiser approaches the dock downwind/-current. The helm is centered, with controls neutral or idle forward as the skipper judges the approach and determines the effect of the current on the vessel. He is prepared to power away from the dock if it appears that the approach will be untenable.

(continued)

(continued)

2. The stern begins to "cock out" as the current pushes the boat down; the skipper compensates by placing his port engine in easy reverse to keep the boat parallel with the dock. Depending on the particular circumstances, wind/current, and reactions of the boat, he will carefully work the helm and throttles to position the boat nearly stationary and parallel to the dock.

3. The boat is now parallel to the dock. Both engines are in easy reverse, the starboard engine is running a few more rpms than the port, and the helm is kicked somewhat to starboard, helping the boat maintain position at a near standstill. Fenders are in place, and the crew stands by with a looped line to hand to a person on the dock.

4. Close alongside, the boat is at bare minimum steerage. The looped dockline is led to the cruiser's midships cleat where it is belayed with a figure-eight turn ready to be eased or tightened by the crew.

5. The dockline has been placed on the cleat by the person on the dock (not shown). Note the figure-eight turn on the midships cleat. The boat's crew will have complete control to adjust the length of the line per captain's orders.

6. The midships line is taken up tightly in as close proximity to the dock cleat as possible. The boat will remain in place until proper docklines can be set up.

Single Screws

These are the steps for docking single screws downwind or downcurrent:

1. Place fenders on the side of the boat that is opposite to the dock. (See photo 1 on the following page.)

2. Have the crew place a line wrapped in a figure eight, but not hitched, to the bow mooring cleat. The line should have a loop on the free end—either a spliced loop or a bowline.

3. Approach, slowly, parallel to the dock about a boat length off.

4. If it is necessary to place the engine in reverse to decrease speed, note that by doing so the prop torque will tend to kick the stern in one direction or another. It is important to know beforehand whether your prop turns to the right or left. Most props on single-screw pleasure vessels are right-hand turning; therefore, when placed in reverse, they will tend to kick the stern to port. If that is the case, be prepared to compensate with the rudder to keep the boat parallel to the dock. If you are operating an outboard or stern drive, make sure the lower unit is centered before hitting reverse. The stern will still kick to port (if the prop is a right-hand-turning one), but you will be able to compensate by turning the wheel in the opposite direction. (See photo 2.)

5. When the bow is opposite the cleat/piling where you want to lay, back hard until there's little or no way on and turn the bow into the dock.

6. Have the crew hand (not toss) the looped end of the line to a person on the dock with instructions to place the loop over the cleat or piling.

7. Place the engine in neutral and center the helm; the current will swing the boat around. Have the crew ease the line around the cleat until the boat is almost opposite the dock in the other direction. Then the crew should take up on the line. As the line is wrapped in a figure eight around the cleat, all the crew needs to do is pull straight up on the line and secure it. Putting another wrap around the cleat or attempting to hitch it is not necessary.

8. If there is no one available on the dock to help, have the crew secure the line to the bow cleat with at least two wraps around the base and a hitch, and place the bow as just discussed. In the instant before the current takes the boat, have your crew step off and wrap the line around the dock cleat as already detailed. As the current swings the boat around, the crew—now on the dock—can adjust the line until the boat lies comfortably alongside. (See photo 3.)

9. Make sure that the crew does not have to jump to the dock. Properly performed, there will be an instant where the bow is against the dock allowing the crew to step ashore. If you are unable to place the bow against the dock go around and try again.

Approaching a dock downwind/-current with a single screw. 1. This single-screw cruiser is approaching the dock downwind/-current. Note how the stern is cocked out as it is set down by the wind and current.

2. While it was the skipper's original intent to bring the boat parallel to the dock, the strength of the current made that impossible. Therefore as the current swung the boat around, he eased the bow toward the dock and directed the crew to step ashore. If there were a dock person available, he would have directed the crew to hand a bow line, belayed to the portside bow cleat, to that dock attendant.

3. The crew has successfully stepped ashore *only because the boat had come to a near stop and it was perfectly safe to do so—the only way this maneuver should be performed.* The looped end of the dockline is on the portside bow cleat, and she has stepped ashore with the bitter end of the line that she belays as a figure eight on the cleat, which allows her to adjust it per the skipper's orders. If there had been a dock attendant available, the looped end would have been sent ashore and the figure eight belayed on the bow cleat and adjusted as per skipper's orders.

4. The current continues to swing the boat around (note the fender in place); the crew adjusts the line as directed by the skipper.

5. The boat continues to come around, now almost bow-in to the wind/current.

6. Alongside the dock, the boat is now ready to have proper lines set up.

Shown here is the same maneuver if there had been a dock person available. The looped line is on the dock (not shown), and crew can control the line—and the boat—by adjusting the line. Note the turn around the horn of the bow cleat to give more control.

Here the looped end is on the dock, and the crew is easing the line out as the boat is set in.

BOW AND STERN THRUSTERS

The current in New York's East River off Pier 11 at the foot of Wall Street can run up to 6 knots on the ebb, but apparently the skipper of the 110-foot yacht shaping up to berth alongside the T of that 900-foot-long pier wasn't going to let a little thing like a rampaging ebb crimp his style. His initial approach looked smart, bow into the current, yacht port side parallel to the dock and about 50 yards off. But he was coming in fast, and when he finally decided to shoot for a landing, he angled his bow in, way in, allowing the full force of the current—now acting on the bow's flat surface instead of the stem—to push it even farther dockside. With a confident smile he punched his bow thruster to push off from the concrete-edged pier.

During the New York minute that the thruster valiantly tried to stem the tide, the skipper, smiling no more, tried to twist free by throwing his port engine into neutral and coming hard astern starboard. It was to no avail as that current in conjunction with the immovable concrete pier head deftly crunched the yacht's aluminum superstructure into that of a thoroughly stomped-on empty soda can.

A decade ago when that incident took place, thrusters, both bow and stern, were big boat items; even that 110-footer was in the smaller range of vessels so equipped. In today's boating world, however, there really is no lower limit on the size of boats that can be equipped with a thruster. (Well, let's be real—below 30 feet or so they're a bit grandiose.) Bow thrusters are by far most common. But it's showtime for stern thrusters, too, not only because of the current popularity of single-screw trawler-type and tugboat look-alike yachts—where thrusters can turn klutzes into pros—but also due to external installation options, such as transom-mounted bolt-on units, where there is no need to chop big holes aft.

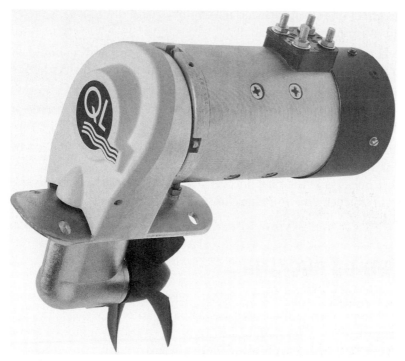

Bow thruster (Volvo).

Thrusters really come into their own when leaving a berth—especially if it's a tight one. Just ask any skipper who has had to pull a yacht out of an end-of-boat-show slip or a crowded restaurant dock when the boss is aboard.

And of course, as with any "gee whiz" technology, the tendency can be to expect too much. For instance, what if the captain of that 110-footer hadn't had a bow thruster? He would have made his approach parallel to the dock backed off until he was just breasting the current at zero speed. Then he would have gently edged the bow in, and as the ebb pushed the bow dockside, he would've thrown his dockside engine into neutral (or somewhat ahead depending on the conditions) and eased astern with his off-dock wheel, and the boat would have nicely parallel parked.

Bow and/or stern thrusters allow the same maneuver, just quicker and more efficiently. If you utilize thrusters with the expectation that they'll get you out of a jam, you're not using them correctly. Here are the keys to using them effectively:

1. The bow thruster allows you to maneuver the bow laterally, but don't make it a contest between a strong current and a powerful thruster. You could lose. The more the bow protrudes into a current, the stronger that current will act upon the broad surface of the boat and the harder the thruster will have to work to counteract it.

2. The stern thruster, also, will ease the stern sideways without utilizing the rudder and astern/forward action of a single screw or the "twist" of a twin. (When using the

sideways effect of a stern thruster, the engine[s] still has to be engaged to maintain fore-and-aft motion.)

3. Whenever using a thruster, mentally review how the maneuver should be performed without the thruster and thus remember that the thruster is an aid, not the main event.

4. When maneuvering with thrusters, especially when entering or exiting a slip, it's best to set your rudder amidships as the action of bow and stern thrusters will be more accentuated to the side on which the rudder is cocked.

5. Whether you are utilizing thrusters are not, when edging bow-first out of a slip, have crew looking forward as the wind and current will grab at your slow-moving bow as soon as it pokes past the pier line. As you do with your radar, practice using that thruster even when you don't have to so you'll be adept when you do need the little sidewinder.

STOP-AND-GO DOCKING

Commercial skippers, tug drivers, crewboat jockeys, ferryboat or excursion vessel captains, and just about anyone else who drives a boat at an hourly wage doesn't have time to waste shaping their vessel up to dock just right when they might have to be under way again in minutes. To the casual observer, they're in and out and about their business without forethought or caution—until you hang around long enough. Then you see there's nothing haphazard about the way they handle their equipment. Everything's thought out in advance, and, usually, the same techniques are used over and over again—practiced moves that *look* easy.

As pleasure boaters, we might not have to board a pilot or relief crew to run out to a waiting tanker, but there are times that you will need to come in to pick up provisions or a six-pack or to drop off a passenger without going through the whole docking procedure. This is stop-and-go docking—coming up to the dock without tying up, usually just long enough to transfer a person or a package. Often, though, when a tug plans a stop-and-go for any reason, he'll nose up to the dock, apply just enough power to keep it there, and with minute rudder adjustments hang out as long as he wants. With these considerations, this action can work for the pleasure set, too:

1. This maneuver shouldn't be practiced in turbulent waters or with fast-moving beam currents; currents directly astern or on the bow can be beneficial.

2. The bow (or dock) must be well fendered. Prepare nylon docking lines in advance by securing them to two bow cleats if they are available; if, as in many boats, there is only one bow cleat, midships cleats can be used. Tie the line in a figure-eight configuration to each cleat without hitching it, as it will be adjusted from on the boat. The lines must be long enough to reach the dock with an additional few feet for adjustment.

3. The boat should be gently nosed into the dock—the boat forms a right angle to the dock—equidistant between two cleats or bollards.

4. The crew sends each line ashore, and it is looped around the corresponding cleat/bollard. The line is tightened from aboard—the figure eights around each cleat are loosened and then the slack is taken in and the lines re-secured.

5. By easing carefully into reverse, the boat is held in place against the bow lines.

Single-Screw Stop-and-Go Docking

On single-screw boats it won't take long to figure out how much rudder to apply to counteract the torque of the prop (the same goes with twins in applying rpm). The advantage here is that it's easy to counteract a beam breeze, and, with care, pulpits and anchors might not get trashed.

1. With strain on the lines and minimal reverse revolutions on the engine, the boat will remain in position. Any beam wind or current can be compensated for by cocking the rudder on a single-screw vessel (or adjusting the rpm on one engine or the other on twins). The helm should never be left unattended.

2. When preparing to disengage, the power should be eased off rather than abruptly closing the throttle(s) as the slingshot effect can force the bow into the dock.

3. Once the tension is off the lines, the boat can be eased into reverse and into the stream.

Twin-Screw Stop-and-Go Docking

The twin-screw crewboat/ferry set favor the following method of backing in to pick up their passengers: the skipper looks like he's blasting in fast but then slows at the last minute before nosing up to the dock gently enough to keep an eggshell intact. But watch closely. The boat actually comes to a full stop—for a split second—10 or 15 yards short of the dock; then it slides in not to shatter the proverbial egg.

1. The trick is to mentally picture the dock as being 10 or 15 yards short of the actual dock. This also tends to counteract any transient depth or distance perception errors that can occur on the water. With a little practice, any boater can look like a pro backing in.

2. It's important to remember that most vessels are more powerful in reverse gear than in forward. Therefore, when engaging forward gear as a brake, it will not be as effective as utilizing the reverse gear when slowing the boat when it's going forward. This method demands practice.

3. When backing with twin engines, forget the rudder. Center it and just use the props for control. (If your boat doesn't have a rudder indicator, manually count the turns in each direction and then mark the wheel at *exact* center; an offset of a degree or so will affect the track.) If equipped with four-stick controls, set the throttles to equal rpm and back utilizing just the shifts.

4. If you must maneuver while backing and due to wind and/or current you will need to apply more power to one engine, ascertain that the tachs are equalized when again backing straight astern.

The Indispensable Midships Cleat

THE DELIVERY SKIPPER'S FAVORITE—especially when he or she needs to fuel up quick and then get on the way—is the midships breast line. This works best when approaching the outside of a T, such as a fuel or transient dock; the only requirement is a securely backed midships cleat, which every boat should have. Just ease up so that cleat is directly opposite the dockside piling or cleat; then tie off so there is little or no slack. The (well-fendered) bow and stern will swing out, but the boat is secure. This method is easiest at floating docks with horn cleats, but it can be used anywhere. It's strictly temporary, giving you time to hop off and secure proper bow, stern, and spring lines.

SPRING LINES: THE DOCKING BOATER'S BEST FRIEND

Most boaters understand that in order to be considered properly tied up, a yacht should be restrained with bow and stern lines and fore-and-aft springs. The forward or bow spring runs from a cleat at the bow of the boat to a piling or cleat on the dock somewhat aft of amidships, while the stern spring emanates from a cleat on the stern quarter and runs forward to a piling or dock cleat. These springs prevent the boat from surging fore-and-aft and compensate for tidal changes. But they are capable of so much more.

When your boat is pinned alongside a dock by the wind, the bow spring can be your ticket out. Just throw off all the other lines, turn the rudder or drive toward the dock, and gently come ahead. The stern will slowly kick out into the wind. When it's far enough off the dock, have somebody free the dock end of the spring and toss it aboard (or if the lines are staying on the dock, uncleat it at the bow and toss it ashore). Then come smartly astern, and, when you're safely off, swing around and be on your way. Make sure you fender the boat where it will come in contact with the dock as you're springing off.

The bow spring is in place, preparing to come ahead to spring off dock. However, before doing so it will be necessary to place a fender between the dock and the boat.

If you're windbound near the end of a T dock, the stern spring can get you off also. Just walk the boat back until the stern is adjacent to the end of the dock, throw off all the lines except the stern spring, and carefully come astern. The bow will swing out. When it's heading safely into the breeze, cast off and power ahead. Again, don't forget that fendering.

Departing with wind on the dock. 1. An aft line is being prepared to spring the boat around the dock. 2. With lines secured, the boat is eased gently astern as it springs around the dock. 3. The skipper is almost ready to cast off and drive effortlessly away from the dock. It is important to secure all lines to avoid prop entanglement.

THE MIDSHIPS CLEAT

I'm one of those boaters who came into twin engines late. I cut my eyeteeth on big single-screw excursion and dinner boats that were built for carrying passengers slowly and inexpensively. Their owners believed that twins were a needless luxury best confined to yachts and other vessels where speed was the primary objective and economy the last. And those beasts weren't driver-friendly, either. Slab-sided, with so much freeboard and windage, the prevailing joke was that if they only had a jib they would give any sailboat a run for its money.

Docking those dinosaurs, however, wasn't as difficult as you might imagine. Virtually all it took was a midships cleat and some basic communication between the line handler and the skipper—a technique that can be used on any single-screw vessel, no matter what the size. That midships cleat is the key to landing a single-screw vessel alongside any dock, regardless of wind or current. Once you get a line on the dock, the boat *will* come in.

If tossing the line ashore isn't practical, try securing one end of a long line to the midships cleat. As you nose in, have your crew walk the line forward and hang a loop of the line over a bollard or dockside cleat, keeping the bitter end in their hands. Then back the boat off and work it until it's parallel to the dock. (Hint: Using a long line gives you more room to maneuver.)

Whichever way you got the end of the line ashore, after the boat is lined up where you want it, tell the crew to take in the slack and pull the line tight under one horn of the midships cleat. They shouldn't cleat it—just hold it there securely by pulling upward. Then have the boat come ahead slowly while steering *away from* the dock. That will keep the bow from pointing in, keeping the boat parallel as it side-slips closer to the dock. When you pass the point on the dock where you wish to berth, come astern and have the crew take in the slack as you go. Shift into forward again and come ahead, repeating the process until you're alongside. Then step ashore and feel like a pro. You can slide *Mom's Mink* into a spot only slightly larger than its overall length that way. Hey, who needs twins?

PAINLESS TIE-UPS

Most of us are intimately acquainted with our slip; we've spent lots of time laying out our springs, breasts, bow, and stern lines of correct lengths and securing them to pilings and dock cleats with carefully pre-tied or spliced loops so they're just right for easy snatching when we ease back in. When pulling into a strange slip on a cruise, however, it sometimes comes as a shock to find that there are no lines ready and waiting—we have to secure ourselves. The consequences of doing it improperly or not quickly enough, especially in a tidal or wind situation and without a dock attendant standing by, can be catastrophic—especially as there's invariably a lawyer-owned gold-plater in the next berth. The following sections explain some tying-up tips that work for me.

1. The midships line is placed on the dock cleat.

2. The onboard and dock cleats are tied as closely together as possible. Where can the boat go?

Here's another neat use of that midships cleat. With a spring line led forward to a cleat on the dock, all the skipper has to do is back easy and give a bit of helm toward the dock and the boat will spring right alongside. Although shown here on a twin-engine outboard, this technique works well with singles or twins, outboards or inboards.

Any line can be easily controlled as long as there is one turn around the horn of the cleat and tension is maintained as the line is eased or let out. This bow line can be pulled in or eased out, the latter allowing it to be used as a spring as the boat is backed down. All the crew needs to do is pull up tightly to stop the boat's rearward progress, or ease the tension to provide more slack.

Endless Loop and Clove Hitch

When backing into a strange slip, I often station a crewmember between amidships and aft with a long line secured to a bow cleat. As the outermost (windward) piling comes by, he passes the line behind the piling and then walks forward as I back in. If the wind is pushing the bow off, he is able to counteract it. When the bow is where I want it, he loops the line around the piling, walks aft, and takes a turn around the midships cleat. Thus I have a temporary bow and forward spring with one line. He or I then hop aft and secure a stern line. We can then secure separate dedicated bow and springs.

If there are no projections on the pilings to keep a looped line from slipping down, I use clove hitches. The advantage of this hitch is that it can be tied from the middle of the piling if it's too high to reach over, or it can be tied while dropping over the top of the piling. The disadvantage of the clove hitch is that for it to work properly there needs to be constant tension on it, so if the boat is going to be there for any length of time the hitch should be doubled and set up very tightly.

Clove hitch. 1. When tying a clove hitch, the line is wrapped around the post/piling and the working end of the line is passed over the standing end. 2. The working end is again wrapped around the piling and placed over itself. 3. Both ends are pulled tight to complete the hitch. *Note:* for the clove hitch to hold securely, a constant strain should be on the line. If this knot is to tie the boat for any length of time, it is best to tie one or two half hitches atop the clove hitch to hold it in place.

The "Choked" Loop

When I need to get a loop on the piling as soon as possible, especially if there is some projection to keep the loop from sliding down, I'll take an existing spliced or knotted loop (it's rarely wide enough to fit over a piling or large mooring cleat) and "choke" it by pushing the standing end of the line through the loop, thus increasing it to any size I want. Not only can the loop be made large enough to fit over any piling or cleat, but with a little practice it can be used as a lasso to snag an out-of-reach piling.

Using a "choked" loop. 1. Captain Skip wants to place a loop around this piling. However, the piling is too high and the loop is too small, so he will "choke" it in place. 2. He places the loop around the piling. 3. Skip takes the standing end of the line and prepares to place it through the loop. 4. He runs the line through the loop and *voila* the loop is around the piling without the toss or climb. 5. Here is the choked loop with the line through it. The loop can be made as wide as there is line available.

Another use of the choked loop is when you need to get a line on an inaccessible piling. 1. Make the loop as wide as possible, and put a couple of coils in your non-throwing hand. Don't forget to hang on to the end. 2. Let her rip. 3. It takes lots of practice. 4. But once you get the hang of it (so to speak), it comes in very handy. It's easy to over-concentrate on this maneuver. Always watch your balance, and never stand on the bow without support. Rose keeps one foot in the bow cockpit and another forward allowing for a sturdy stance.

Cleats and Bitts

If this hasn't happened to you, you're either a better boater or a bigger liar than me. You have a wrap around a mooring or dockside cleat either as a spring or securing line and you put the strain to it. Suddenly that nice figure eight that you tied begins negotiating its way around the cleat until it, and the boat, go their separate ways. This "oops" factor is usually preceded by a diminishing of the diameter of the (usually) nylon braided line as it reacts to the pull. We can't fault the line. By its nature, nylon, as well as having stretch and spring—which makes it suitable for mooring and anchoring rodes—is a slippery beast, especially when it's braided. (Three-strand nylon affords somewhat more friction, but I wouldn't recommend against braided as it's stronger, prettier, and easier to splice.)

We can, however, look to our belaying technique—and to the cleats that we're tying off to. I believe the ideal cleat is the horn type with the projections of the horn extending far enough from the base so that there's room for at least one and ideally two full turns around the base before making the figure eight. It's the turns around the base that provide most of the holding power with the figure eight(s) followed by the final half hitch (it's correct if the final turn lies parallel to the first cross over) that affords the ultimate security. I like that cleat to be high enough off the deck so I can wrap enough line of sufficient diameter for the particular boat.

Unfortunately, the traditional horn cleat has done in enough toes to warrant special recognition in the Orthopedist's Hall of Fame. Consequently, builders have come up with pop-up, folding, gently curved, and various other politically and anatomically correct devices to ease the pain. No matter the design, all cleats must have the ability to take those necessary round turns, figure eights, and hitches.

Bitts, also known as samson posts, are tied the same way except in the vertical plane instead of the horizontal. Their advantages are that there is usually room for additional round turns around the base before the figure eights (finished off with a half hitch, of course) around the projecting pins.

So-called "Eurostyle" cleats—two upward angling posts from a common base—are often seen on larger boats. The trick with these is to wrap the round turns (two, three, or more) around one base before weaving the figure eight (topped by the half hitch, also applied to one post) between the posts. Round turns around both posts can slip under strain with the usual concomitant embarrassment.

A horn cleat tied with a half hitch.

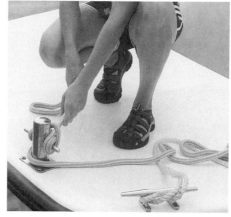

A samson post with a hitch in place. One can place a turn or two of line around the base of the post to allow easy control over boat position against the dock before tying it off.

This is a curved, horn-style dock cleat with a choked loop in place.

This bow cleat is sufficiently high off the deck to allow the line to be securely looped upon itself. The disadvantage of belaying line in this manner is that the line will be difficult to remove under strain.

A commercial-style samson post on a towboat.

Recessed cleats are less likely to foul against dockside obstructions.

Horn cleats with rings are rarely seen on modern boats.

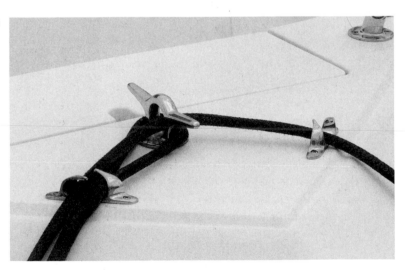

2

Confidence on Open Water

DECIDING WHAT OPEN-WATER maneuvers are advanced can be a close call in itself. I've chosen situations that can be fraught with anxiety, such as transferring a person from one boat to another at sea, losing an engine, or facing the threat of imminent collision. In these situations, the boater can benefit from knowing some established procedures—recipes to follow, if you will—that replace guesswork with proven methods.

RUNNING AT SPEED

A few years ago, alongside the usual navigational buoys along Connecticut's Thames River, stood a brand new 45-foot go-fast. It was brazenly ensconced atop a jetty, which was usually submerged at low tide. The boat reposed peacefully, and incongruously, there for a few days until the authorities figured out how to remove it. The boat's skipper had swerved sharply to avoid a "strange object," which turned out to be an innocent nun buoy that had been in the same place for that past fifteen years that this guy had been cruising the river. The only difference was his past cruising had been considerably slower than the 75 mph his new muscle boat was running at the time of the accident.

This story illustrates a few points to keep in mind when we slam the hammer down. First, at speed everything changes. Yes, it's one of those things we know intellectually. But driving fast is a matter of instinct, reflexes, and habits, which are independent of intellect. The person who mounted that jetty knew everything was going to happen faster, but his habits and instinct predominated. When that nun showed up, he didn't recognize it;

it wasn't where his brain thought it would be. Therefore, he reacted instantly by swerving to escape the perceived danger—right into real trouble, onto the jetty.

Professional racers recognize that familiar waters at moderate speeds become strange worlds at high ends. They study the course and run it frequently, faster and faster until it and the corresponding landmarks and buoys become familiar at all speeds.

The pros also recognize that at speed boats react differently than they do in cruising mode. Their credo is: The only thing that should go fast in a go-fast is the boat. In other words, you shouldn't initiate any sudden maneuvers. A quick yank at the wheel could send a boat off to parts unknown (or onto a nearby jetty). The trick here is to train your right hand—the throttle hand—to react first. Any question about what's ahead, or any possibility that the boat is headed into danger, should result in a reduction of power rather than a sudden change of direction—and even that reduction should be done gradually. (Boats have been sunk by the stern wave washing over the transom after an abrupt decrease in speed.)

The skipper of a powerboat who spends time cruising on plane, especially when there are guests aboard, needs to keep in mind that a vessel on plane is a carefully balanced machine and any factor—weight distribution or taking a sea or wake—can upset that balance.

Crossing Boat Wakes

The subject of crossing boat wakes is clouded by two common misconceptions: (1) cutting wakes can be routinely performed without backing down or dropping off plane and (2) wakes should be taken head-on, at a 90-degree angle or thereabouts. In fact, the safest method to cut a wake is to back off plane and swing into the oncoming wake, taking it at somewhat less than 90 degrees to avoid the sudden decrease in speed and the "slam" that can result from a direct, right-angle hit.

When approaching another boat's wake, it's safer to "cut" a wake (take it at somewhat of an angle) than to take it on your beam. A boat on plane—and thus already on the edge of stability—that encounters a wake on the beam, can, depending on factors like the size of the wake and the size and speed of the boat encountering it, experience a momentary loss of control or, in a worst-case scenario, broach or even capsize. To cut the wake safely, it's important to back off plane and look around carefully before making your cut. For instance, some years back, a boater on Lake Michigan cut a wake from a passing boat without backing off or looking around and was T-boned by a third boat.

A cutting vessel that remains on plane is flirting with disaster. The boat's heel as it swings into the turn compromises its balance, while cutting the wake at any angle less than a right angle at the same time will further decrease its stability. (I know that second part seems to contradict a statement that I made just a few sentences back, but bear with me here.) Throw in other factors—a sudden, unexpected passenger weight redistribution; a larger wake than expected; or a gust of wind—and the boat can slalom out of control or capsize.

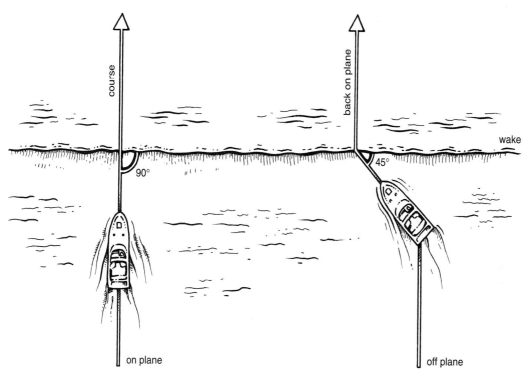

When cutting a wake at speed (not recommended), take it at a 90-degree angle (left). The preferred approach (right) is to slow down, drop off plane, and cut the wake at an angle of roughly 45 degrees before getting back on course and on plane.

The contradiction here is that a 90-degree cut *is* preferable in that it lessens the possibility of a dangerous heel, but at the same time it increases the risk of going airborne, "stuffing" the bow into the next wave, and/or landing so hard that you break something on the boat or throw yourself or a passenger off balance. And if you're doing it at high speed, as the deep-V and performance sets argue you should, any miscalculation in the angle of approach could trigger the instability described above. The higher the speed, and the higher the wake, the more important it is that the cut take place at that optimum right angle.

Bottom line: the best, most prudent approach is to slow down, drop off plane, and take wakes at a shallow angle. (In other words, depending on the size of your boat and the approaching wake [little boat + big wake = slow way down], take the wake somewhat forward of the beam at an angle from 25 to 45 degrees. After you take the first few, you'll quickly figure out what works best.) However, if you and your guests are in it for the rush, and you're really determined to take it on plane and at speed, cut the wake as close to 90 degrees as possible.

Using Trim Tabs

In addition to their weather-beaten mugs and the whiskers sprouting out of their ears, you can always spot traditionalist skippers by their disdain for newfangled devices like bow thrusters, trim tabs, and porcelain thrones. Okay, I'm of that set, and while I deep-sixed the galvanized bucket and opted for the porcelain throne years ago, it's been relatively recently that I learned to appreciate thrusters. That happened when a quick push from the little sidewinders kept me from re-designing a gold-plater while pulling out of a micro-berth in Ft. Lauderdale. I became a proponent of trim tabs upon discovering that a touch of tab can make a jostling offshore jaunt almost pleasant even when breasting a head sea aboard a battlewagon.

The trouble with tabs is that they have bad PR. Many boaters, including some pros, will tell you that they hardly use them, except maybe to compensate for poor weight distribution or to straighten out a chine walk in a stiff breeze. The fact is tabs can and should be used for a lot of purposes, including blasting out of the hole, trimming for fuel efficiency, and ensuring an easier offshore ride. Some sport boat and performance-oriented, narrow-beamed cruiser aficionados prefer a bow-down running angle as the steering tends to be more sensitive and the boat more responsive. That's not a good idea. Not trimmed properly, most powerboats—especially those with deep-V hulls—will be more susceptible to oversteering and possible loss of control, including "stuffing" the bow into a sea or a wake at somewhat of a downward angle. This can stop the boat dead, throwing its occupants forward out of their seats and causing injuries. It can also result in swamping.

The most common use of trim tabs is to correct for list to port or starboard, due to wind conditions, prop torque, or improper weight distribution. Of course, trim tab deployment (down tab on the side of the list) will straighten the boat out, but that deployed tab creates drag that affects speed and fuel efficiency. You can't change the wind (although it will change either of its own volition or when you turn, and when you do turn you'll need to be quick on the tab to straighten the boat and avoid *over*trimming), but you can load your boat properly to avoid a list. Also, if you're constantly trimming to compensate for torque, you might want to chat with your prop guy regarding a change in specs.

While inboards primarily utilize trim tabs, the outboard and I/O set can benefit from them as well—especially if you're into offshore jumps. Sure, an outboard's power trim can adjust the boat's fore-and-aft attitude, but you're asking a lot of that prop. It's not only pushing the boat forward but also pushing the stern up or down to adjust the trim, which is inefficient and wastes fuel. Furthermore, power trim can't correct a boat's list, and at slower speeds it is not very effective at changing the boat's trim in any case. If you're using that power trim often, it might pay to install tabs.

Getting back to inboards: trim tabs are basically add-ons. A well-designed, moderate-V, relatively heavy cruiser will rarely need them. As long as the payload is properly distributed and the boat sits evenly on its lines, it shouldn't take on a list while under way that

trim tab   trim tab

Trim tabs do more than just correct for uneven trim. They can help get you up on plane quicker and maintain a more comfortable ride in rough conditions. (Formula)

would require tabs. A moderate-V design reduces the possibility of "chine-walking," or leaning into a beam breeze, that a more extreme deep-V hull can be prone to. I know of one long-established, top-end boatbuilder who views tabs with disdain and claims they have never sullied any of his yachts. However, when tabs are available, they can enhance the boating experience—especially with smaller and lighter boats. Here are a few tips on their proper use:

- Prior to going on plane, when the boat is dead in the water or going at slow speed, place the trim tabs in the "up" or bow-up position. At that position they are tucked against the boat's hull and not in use. As you advance the throttle to bring the boat up to planing speed, the stern will begin to "squat" and the bow will rise. At that time hit the "bow-down" tab switch, thus adjusting the tabs down, which will push the stern up and the bow down. Some boaters will not use the tabs until the boat is on plane; however, by tabbing bow-down after increasing speed but prior to achieving planing speed, the engine won't work so hard and you'll plane out quicker.

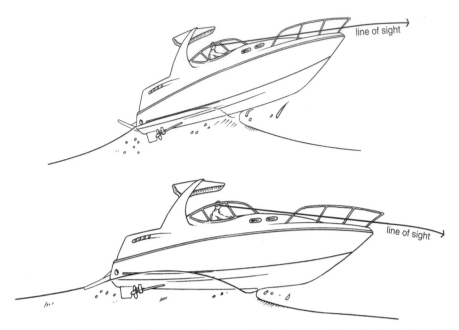

When trying to get on plane with no trim tabs, or tabs in the up position (top), the bow lifts and the skipper cannot see forward. Deploying the tabs (bottom) brings the bow down, gets the boat on plane faster, and provides the skipper with a good line of sight.

- When you do trim, "tweak" the switch in little increments. This will help avoid over-trimming—excessive bow down—which can give the boat that "ice skating" feel or an oversensitivity to helm movements. If that happens, switch bow up until the boat settles in.

- In head seas, again incrementally trim the bow down somewhat, giving the boat time to respond. The bow is designed to cut through seas. By trimming bow down, your boat will take the seas on the sharp edge of the stem rather than lower down where it begins to flatten out. It'll ride smoother with less pounding.

- Conversely, when running down sea, keep the tabs tucked in. The boat will track easier, and the stern won't sashay around as much. In flatter water, relatively light aft-weighted cruisers like sportfishermen will tend to ride somewhat bow-high if untrimmed. Trimming down not only makes for a more comfortable ride but will increase fuel economy.

RUNNING A TWIN ON ONE WHEEL

Among the advantages of twin screws is that if one engine goes down, you can tool home on the other. Well, yes and no. For example, while bringing it up the coast, I lost an engine on a late-model 35-footer with twin props. Okay, we were only 30 miles out; so turn around and return.

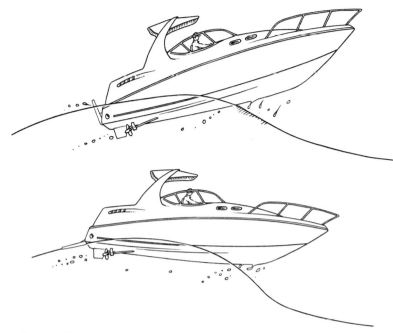

Going into head seas without the tabs deployed (top), the bow is about to slam into the trough as the wave passes astern. Tabs down (bottom) keeps the bow down, reducing slamming. Tabs must be deployed incrementally, the proper position being determined by the boat's behavior and crew comfort.

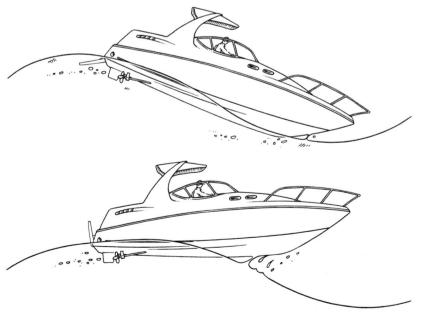

Tabs down in following seas (top) may cause the bow to dig into the next wave. With the tabs up (bottom), the bow will be more likely to lift to the wave.

But that was easier said than done. The boat wouldn't move away from the dead prop, the starboard engine was out, and we couldn't turn to port. A 3-foot sea and stiff quartering breeze were complicating factors. To get started back, we had to "wear ship," turn to starboard past 180 degrees until we found our return course.

I've run into this situation before; relatively close prop placement and narrow beam are contributing factors. Generally speaking, the narrower the beam, the closer the prop placement and the less efficient the remaining prop will be in turning the boat away from the dead prop. If the port prop is down, the inclination of the starboard prop is to turn the boat to port—toward the dead prop. Depending on the design of the boat and the conditions, turning away from the dead prop will, at best, result in a significantly greater turning radius; at worst, the boat will not be able to turn away from the dead prop at all, resulting in the need to "wear ship," as mentioned above. The way I deal with it—after I quit cussing designers who think their computer-aided design (CAD) programs are suitable replacements for adequate sea trials—is to take the following steps:

- Back off and forget about making time.
- Tab up to keep the stern down. If there's moveable weight, get it aft; more stern in the water will allow a better bite, thus more positive steerage.
- If there are seas running, use them to your advantage. For instance, if taking seas forward of the beam, ease off as the boat meets a sea on the side of the working propeller; that lessens its tendency to push the boat off course. Power up upon meeting a sea on the side of the downed prop. Add power and make course changes in the troughs where resistance is least. If there is little sea running, there should be no problem as most boats should be able to work away from that dead prop in flat water.
- Make for the nearest port. Even though the boat is progressing comfortably, the downed engine cuts your safety margin in half.
- Perform frequent engine checks while under way. The single engine is working harder and is more likely to overheat or throw a belt.
- Try not to allow the nonpowered shaft to freewheel. Doing so can cause transmission damage since transmission oil is not being circulated. Depending on the transmission, sometimes freewheeling can be prevented just by placing the engine in gear. More often the shaft will need to be physically restrained.

Restraining the Shaft

How to restrain the shaft will vary depending on the installation. You may be able to wedge the shaft or the shaft coupling against a hull stringer or the sides of the shaft tunnel with wooden wedges, if these are available. (Make a note for your shopping list, and keep a few in your emergency supplies on board.) Or try clamping and securing a pipe wrench or Vise-Grips tool around the shaft. When gripping the shaft by this means, be careful not to score the shaft. There cannot be metal-to-metal contact; a wood or fabric buffer must be placed between the jaws of the tool and the shaft. It might be possible to place a box-end wrench on one of the bolts of the shaft/transmission coupling and wedge the opposite end of the wrench against a stringer or the hull. In some cases, the shaft/transmission coupling can be disconnected, which will allow the shaft to free-wheel, but will protect the transmission from damage. Examine the situation carefully, however, before you take this route. On some older installations, there is a possibility that by detaching the shaft at the transmission coupling, the shaft can slide out through the stuffing box. If this possibility exists, disconnecting the shaft should not be attempted.

AVOIDING COLLISIONS

When I ran excursion and sightseeing cruises on New Jersey's Barnegat Bay, it was on holiday weekends that I became a fervent believer in boater education—especially Fourth of July weekends. On those weekends, the bay would froth with the antics of the ill-informed, the hostile, and the clueless. Boats would approach—fast—from the port, starboard, ahead, and astern. The Rules of the Road (formally known as the International Regulations for the Prevention of Collision at Sea, or COLREGS) would cycle through my mind as I watched the rules torpedoed. And, of course, there were always the meandering sailboats demanding with near-biblical justification their right-of-way.

Sadly, I witnessed an accident that totaled both boats and resulted in five people in the water (none with life jackets on) as a sailboat realized, too late, that a speeding motorboat wasn't going to change course. Although the driver of the powerboat took evasive action, it also was just a bit too late. No thanks to either operator—or the non-life-jacket-clad passengers—there were no fatalities or serious injuries—and that was only because of the quick response of the surrounding vessels. Picture that situation when you study the Rules of the Road and determine which Rules were broken by both operators. (Hint: There were at least three.)

The sad truth remains, however, that if you are involved in an accident, even through no fault of your own, you can be held at least partially responsible. Attribute that to the one Rule that supersedes all the others. It's called the General Prudential Rule—Rule 2(b):

> In construing and complying with these rules due regard shall be had to all dangers of navigation and collision and to any special circumstances, including the limitations of the vessels involved, *which may make a departure from these rules necessary to avoid immediate danger* [my emphasis].

In a nutshell: if you're the privileged vessel and you doggedly maintain course and speed until some yahoo T-bones you, you share the blame.

Through time, I have developed a survival strategy that covers many different situations, allowing me to make instant decisions when necessary that, generally, will keep me legal and still avoid having to fall back on Rule 2(b).

- Let's begin with that perennial nemesis, the meandering sailboat. Yes, it has the right-of-way, but the Rules also state that the privileged vessel (the sailboat) is required to maintain its course and speed. Therefore, when he tacks in front of you does he lose his privileged status? Probably. I've seen powerboaters who, believing that, wait until the last moment—maybe hoping to teach the erroneous sailor a "lesson"—before giving way. That's inviting of an accident, especially when running at planing speed where it's easy to miscalculate how slow that sailboat really is. I give way long before we approach middle-finger-waving range.

- The most frequent near-collision scenarios I've observed occur when two powerboats are on a nose-to-nose collision course. The Rules (and common sense) state that both boats should turn to starboard. That turn should not be a gradual one. Too often, the drift to the right of one boat isn't noticed soon enough by the other. If safety allows, I make a distinct and sharp move to starboard. I want the other guy to know that I am changing course.

- In high-speed crossing situations, decisions often have to be made quickly. As a rule of thumb, I imagine that if it were dark would I be able to see his running light? If the boat is to my starboard and I can see his port bow (red running light), I know he has right of way and I'll give way. If he's to my port, I'm the starboard boat; I would see green and he would see red. Therefore, I'm the privileged vessel and he should give way.

- Now, common sense comes into play. Does he know the Rules? I always assume not and watch him closely. If it looks like he is not going to give way, I do. I check traffic, back off, and turn away (to starboard) from him. I have seen accidents occur by privileged vessels that stubbornly hold course and increase speed to pass ahead of the offending boat or that turn into the other boat's direction hoping to encourage him to veer off. Even if the privileged vessel does nothing but maintain course and speed, when an accident occurs, the Coast Guard will invariably proportion a degree of blame to the privileged skipper on the assumption that he did not do everything possible to avoid a collision (Rule 2[b]).

- We all know that the Rules require a privileged vessel to maintain course and speed and a vessel being overtaken is always privileged. All things being equal, however, what has worked for me is when the passing boat is not directly astern and my actions will not affect other traffic—I back off. I want that boat to get by me and on his way as quickly as possible. I know that both vessels in a passing situation are at their most vulnerable the longer they are in close proximity—running beam-to-beam. The skippers are restricted in visibility and in maneuverability should the unforeseen occur. Yes, technically it is against the Rules, but I believe it's safer and an exercise in good seamanship and courtesy to back off when being passed.

Taking Bearings

Whenever possible take bearings of an approaching vessel to determine if the possibility of a collision exists. The traditional method of taking bearings is to view the other boat through a handheld compass or your primary compass. If the bearing does not change appreciably, you and the other vessel are on a collision course. However, a compass is not necessary for a bearing. The other boat can be lined up with a stanchion, windshield post, or any fixed object aboard. The bearing—the relationship between that object and the other vessel—must change steadily and appreciably to avoid collision. If the other vessel is a large one and relatively close, the bearing might change and the possibility of collision can still exist. If there is any chance of collision, whether you are the right-of-way vessel or not, you must make every effort to avoid a collision.

Avoiding Collisions Electronically

Most offshore vessels carry one or two VHF radios with a scanning feature that allows continuous coverage of Channels 9, 13, and 16. While Channel 16 is the mandatory distress and calling channel, Channel 9 is used as an alternative calling channel. Channel 13 is a ship-to-ship channel and is monitored by most commercial vessels. Although not required for pleasure boats, it is highly recommended that most vessels monitor Channel 16. If a boater determines that the possibility of collision exists, an attempt at communication with the other vessel should be made on Channel 16. If the other vessel is commercial,

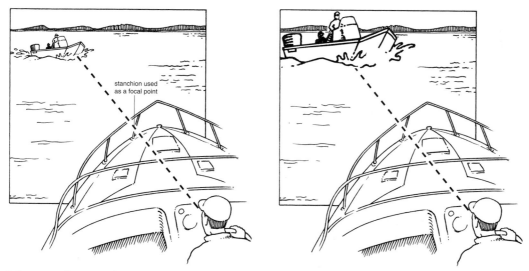

stanchion used
as a focal point

When another vessel is on a crossing course with yours, take a bearing between the vessel and a windshield support or stanchion on your own boat. If that bearing doesn't change appreciably as you continue to approach each other, you're on a collision course.

it should be called on Channel 13. Once communication is established, a procedure to avoid the possibility of collision can be discussed.

A hypothetical discussion should include the following components:

- The calling vessel should identify itself by its location, its type of vessel (motoryacht, etc.), and its heading, and should address the other vessel in similar terms, to the extent possible. If offshore, you should identify locations by latitude and longitude. If inshore, name a geographic landmark or a nearby aid to navigation. For example: "This is the motoryacht *My Boat* at (latitude/longitude) calling the tanker at (latitude/longitude)." Or "This is the motoryacht *BigBoat* approaching Buoy Green 3, southbound in the Intracoastal Waterway calling the tug with barge under tow proceeding northbound off Nearby Point. . . ."

- Once contact is established, the calling vessel can suggest a passing agreement: "Captain, how about a (port-to-port; starboard-to-starboard) meeting."

- It is important that the operator of the other vessel agree with the suggestion before any change of course is initiated: "That's fine, Skipper. Port-to-port will do."

- If the other vessel doesn't reply with an agreement, or if he suggests a passing arrangement contrary to what was originally suggested, the Rules of the Road state that you must sound the danger signal (five blasts on your horn) and stop your boat, as a passing agreement has not been reached and the possibility of collision exists.

- GPS (global positioning system) can be an important aid when communicating with the other vessel, as it enables both vessels to state their position in relation to each other and to determine that they are indeed the vessels involved in the discussion. For instance: "This is the southbound white express cruiser at latitude 27°39' N, longitude 82°53' W calling the eastbound ship about 3 miles ahead of me."

- Radar can complement the GPS as it allows the visualization of the target vessel, and changes in relative bearing between the affected vessels can be immediately noted. (The manuals that accompany radar units include instructions for obtaining relative bearings between two vessels and between the radar-equipped vessel and a target on land.) With this additional radar data at hand, the VHF call can be even more specific: "This is the southbound white express cruiser at latitude 27°13' N, longitude 82°53' W calling the ship on a course of 93 degrees true at latitude 27°35' N and longitude 83°55' W." Once the ship replies, you can negotiate a passing arrangement with him, such as: "Good morning, Captain; would one whistle work for you?" (You are voicing the whistle signal that you would give for the maneuver you are suggesting—passing astern of the ship. A good idea anyway, as the ship being the starboard vessel, has the right-of-way.) The other vessel must agree to your suggestion, "That's fine, Skipper, one whistle is agreed."

Be aware that commercial fishermen often live in their own world of noncommunication or will monitor only those VHF channels that they have previously agreed upon with other fishermen. There's been many times that I've tried to raise them on the radio with no

This working lobster boat and all commercial vessels should be given a wide berth.

success, and the half-dozen times or so in the past few years that I've had close encounters of the wrong kind—near collisions—they have been with non-responsive commercials. If I get an ominous radar target that doesn't respond, I know I've found another one. Best bet? Forget the legalities and try to determine what they're doing and stay well clear. Also stay clear of headboats and drift and bottom fishermen. Non-moving or slow moving radar targets are a dead giveaway that you're looking at a fisherman—so be aware.

TRANSFERRING PASSENGERS OR GOODS AT SEA

Back when I was just getting my feet wet in this business, I was the junior member of a five-man crew delivering a converted sub-chaser from Jacksonville, Florida, to Newport, Rhode Island. On the way, we decided to do some sightseeing in New York and run up through the East River. Just past the city, we spotted a puff of smoke to port that turned out to be a Chris Craft Constellation exploding at a fuel dock. The blast pushed the burning boat off the dock until it grounded a couple of hundred yards offshore. By that time we had worked in close enough to be enveloped by clouds of greasy black smoke—and to spot four people on the foredeck. Our bow towered over their deck, precluding an easy pickup that way, so we tried backing in to take them on the fantail, but 10 yards off our props began chewing up the bottom. Undeterred, our skipper—a retired Navy PT boat commander—spun that 110-footer around, put the bow against the Chris's bow, and lowered the mate—another ex-Navy guy—aboard with a sack full of life preservers and a coil of line. He put the life jackets on and secured the line to the castaways, and, one by one, we hauled them in.

Whenever I've been party to a transfer from one boat to another—fortunately, never again under those circumstances—I've thought of that incident. And one of the lessons I took home from it was that nothing our skipper did was off the cuff—every move he made was done with forethought and knowledge of the exact capabilities of his vessel. Sure, he acted fast, but not without thinking it through first. We might need to come alongside another vessel for pleasure, in the event of an emergency, or to transfer people or goods for one reason or another. It's something that most of us don't do often, so when we undertake such a procedure, the odds are it'll be a learning process as we're doing it.

It helps to be aware of your boat's performance when maneuvering in tight quarters under various wind and sea conditions. Single-screw boats, for example, will favor one direction when turning and backing. Right-turning props will contribute to a tighter turn to starboard coming ahead and kick the stern to port going astern. Counterrotating twins tend to cancel each other out when they're both turning the same rpms, but some boats with twins favor a particular turning radius. All boats have quirks under varying conditions; determine what they are. (See Chapter 1.)

Safe Transfers

Through the years, I've developed these tips for ensuring a safe transfer:

- Never attempt a passenger transfer without adequate crew for helping hands at least on the receiving vessel, and preferably on both.

- Never make a passenger transfer attempt in any kind of foul weather.

- What looks simple 100 yards off can become dicey when the boats are a few feet away and there are swells, wakes, or seas to contend with. Needless to say, the approach has to be slow, bare steerageway at best. The quick kick forward or astern that works so well when coming into your home berth will only create destabilizing turbulence when maneuvering next to another boat.

- It's easier to judge distances between vessels when both boats slowly close the distance beam-to as opposed to bow-to-bow or stern-to-stern. Even when crew is placed at the bow or stern to advise the skipper, a swell can cause damaging contact. Boats approaching beam-to can veer off easier.

- A swim platform–to–swim platform transfer only *appears* ideal. In practice, it should never be attempted in conditions more severe than a slight swell. It's all too easy for one platform to come down on top of the other, with severe consequences to property and passenger.

- As you approach the other vessel, if there is any kind of swell or sea running, try not to place parts of the two boats that are of equal height adjacent to each other. For instance, flybridges, tuna towers, or pulpits can slam into each other due to an unexpected swell.

- Rather than transferring from cockpit to cockpit of equal heights, it is often easier and safer to make the transfer from the (higher) bow of one boat to the (lower) stern of the other. If there is any doubt about the agility or ability of the person climbing from the bow of one boat to the stern of the other, a safety line tended by a crewmember on the bow is a good idea. This can be simply a bow line looped under the passenger's arms. No transfer should ever be attempted without a dedicated crewmember overseeing the transfer on each boat.

- People tend to misjudge distances when leaping from one side deck to another, especially if there is a roll or if the boats are out of synch riding the swells. Do not perform the passenger transfer unless the person can step—not jump—between the boats.

- At the instant of the switch, engines should be in neutral for obvious reasons and not engaged until the transferee is secured. We don't want to toss them back when the boat lurches forward.

- When it is necessary to secure the two boats together, as when transferring goods or an injured passenger, fender the daylights out of them and then run fore and aft spring lines between them to reduce fore-and-aft movement. Do not use breast lines (lines that "cross the gap" go directly from one boat to the other) as they can cause undue strain on the attachments and actually slingshot the boats together.

- When rough seas make it unfeasible to perform the transfer directly from boat to boat, do what the Navy and Coast Guard prefer—put the personnel in an inflatable and haul, row, or motor them over. Often it's easier to transfer people from dinghy to mother ship than ship to ship.

- When contemplating any transfer of personnel offshore, think long and hard as to why one must abandon a perfectly good boat that isn't sinking.

3

Handling Rough Weather

A few years ago, I contracted to bring a 25-foot center console from Norfolk, Virginia, to Cape May, New Jersey. It was a fast, tough boat that worked for me because it was the fall delivery season and I was in an all-fired rush to get the job done so I could dash up to Newport and bring a gold-plater down to West Palm. There was a small craft advisory, but the brunt of the weather wasn't due for another 24 hours and by then I'd be home free and headed to Rhode Island for the big bucks.

We were a few miles into the open Atlantic, not long after clearing the Chesapeake Bay Bridge/Tunnel, when the aptly named Delmarva Coast—where the contiguous shore of Delaware, Maryland, and Virginia form a long, inhospitable stretch—disappeared in a string of squalls. The immediate picture looked equally lousy. A thick haze made it appear that we were running in our own gray world. It was a swerving world as the boat began fishtailing on plane amidst rising seas pushed by an increasing southerly breeze from astern. I knew from past experience that "fishtailing" in following seas—the boat's stern swerving from port to starboard—is an indicator that the boat is going too fast for the conditions. Then, along with the weather, our situation began deteriorating. My partner, John, had gotten up to secure some loose gear at the same time a white-capped sea gave us a violent twist; John's feet slid out from under him and his head slammed into a rod holder, opening up a 2-inch gash over his eyebrow. I immediately backed off. The boat came down off plane, and while the motion was still extreme—quickly up and down as the seas passed underneath us—it wasn't the violent fishtailing that you get when running on plane in a following sea. I took advantage of the eased motion to get a compress on John's wound and take stock of the overall situation, which wasn't improving. I decided to way-point a route back to Norfolk.

It took us three times as long to return to Norfolk as it took to get to the point where we decided to turn back. But we did it fright-free even though that system had turned into a full-blown gale by the time we got between the Chesapeake capes. Now, John has a scar that he thinks makes him look debonair, and I was reminded that a 24-hour forecast is just that—a prediction, not a statement of fact.

Here are a few other lessons I'd forgotten—and relearned that day:

- *The sea doesn't give a hoot about your schedule.*

- *Deteriorating conditions are evident a lot later when you're running with the weather than if you're running upwind or crosswind. It figures. When you're pounding into wind and seas, your rattling back teeth will tell you to slow down a lot sooner than if you're keeping pace with the waves, or even if you're allowing them to pass beneath your hull in the same direction of travel. By the time the crew of a vessel that's running with the wind or the seas realizes what's going on, it might be too late to turn around safely.*

Often, the decision to turn back is prompted by an incident that reflects the danger of the moment, a near broach, green water coming over the transom, or an injury on board. Then the skipper just wants to turn around and head for home as quickly as possible. Your gut reactions, however, may get you into serious trouble, so do nothing without careful planning.

If you decide to initiate a 180-degree turn, please overcome the urge to do so immediately. More often than not, you'll see that waves run in sequences—one, two, three at a time—that can be timed. There will be moments when there will be discernible and well-defined troughs; that's the time to kick it around.

Sometimes, however, it pays just to sit tight. An extreme and fast-moving system will probably pass quickly, and all you need to do is survive. You can do that by using just enough power to keep the bow into the seas and giving up any thought of heading home until the conditions ease. Often, due to the speed of the system, the seas don't have time to build and are not in proportion to the wind velocity. I once got caught in a 2-hour, 40-knot squall (in another center console, love those boats) but the seas never exceeded 4 feet.

BE PREPARED FOR BAD WEATHER

Weather happens. Sure, you can check the forecast and avoid most storms if most of your boating is inland or along a shore, but sooner or later, you're bound to be caught out, so you'd better be prepared to deal with it. And there's a lot you *can* do to be prepared, ranging from having the right gear aboard and making sure the boat is shipshape, to taking specific measures when you know you're going to get hit—the proverbial "battening down of the hatches."

Gear to Have Aboard

I was backing into a berth and, just outside the pier line, slipped both gearshifts into forward to arrest my motion astern. But instead of the click of a positive detent, there was the snap of a broken set screw as the port gear control lever freewheeled on its shaft. Now I had one engine in forward and the other in reverse and a very vulnerable swim platform twisting dangerously close to a concrete piling. Not to worry. I reached into my helm-side tool kit, extracted a pair of Vise-Grips pliers, and clamped them on the control lever shaft. Presto—a new gear shift was born. And that was possibly the umpteenth time in close to 30 years that my little add-on kit saved the day.

In Chapter 8 is a selection of tools that should be aboard any pleasure boat. But of course, they usually end up buried somewhere, especially when you need one. Other than the Leatherman multi-tool that lives on my belt, I always keep within arm's reach the following items in a small roll-up pouch. (You'll have your own tool preferences, but it is important to keep them immediately available because those concrete pilings come up fast.)

- Vise-Grips—the real thing from Irwin Tools, not a knock-off—three of them, the large jaw, curved jaw and needle-nose
- Flat- and Phillips-head screwdrivers
- A roll of 14-gauge marine grade electrical wire, a few crimp connectors, and a crimper/wire cutter

The following pieces of equipment won't fit in a pouch, but they should be nearby as all come in handy in a pinch.

- The lowly galvanized bucket. Why a *galvanized* bucket? Because hardly any boat carries one anymore, opting instead for the ubiquitous plastic model that's not nearly as

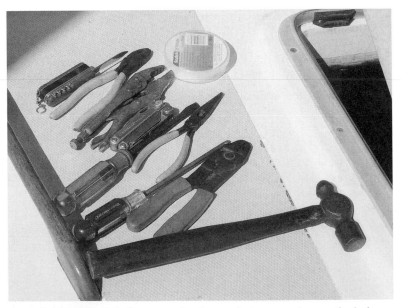

A professional captain keeps a selection tools in a pouch near the helm at all times.

functional. You can bend a stout line to a steel bucket and scoop water even while under way; try that too often with your plastic bucket and it'll be gone. You can load a galvanized bucket with oily rags, set it ablaze, and get attention in an emergency with the plume of black smoke that you'll create with little flame. A small runabout can use it as a drogue to ease steering and increase control in following seas (see later in this chapter for more on drogues and sea anchors). And you can still use it to wash down your decks.

- Parachute cord available from any Army/Navy store—lots of it. I always carry a couple of hundred feet aboard; it'll all stow in a small drawer. It's useful for tie-downs, securing loose gear (always double knot as it is also slippery), and temporary repairs. And, it is so cheap it won't break your heart to cut it or lose it.

- Portable waterproof VHF and GPS transceivers with extra batteries.

- At least two portable, compressed-gas air horns.

- A variety of flashlights, including waterproof units and units that are activated by immersion as well as extra batteries for all devices.

- A few cans of soup and packages of long-term meals ready-to-eat (MREs, military rations). These can go a long way toward boosting the moral of a crew delayed by bad weather. They will store for long periods and can be part of the boat's onboard equipment to be replaced annually.

- Boathooks—not one but two. They're inexpensive and, according to the "Reininger Research Institute," nothing gets lost overboard more frequently than boathooks, except maybe fenders. I like to stow them on deck, one port, one starboard, well secured but ready for a quick grab and release. These are good, stout sticks, and they have many possible uses other than the obvious ones. For example, I've used a pair to jury-rig a sea anchor by duct-taping them into an X and lashing canvas from a cut-up bimini to them with parachute cord.

- A couple of sharp knives, other than galley-ware. This is not just a sailor thing; I've seen the lack of a knife be responsible for serious damage to a yacht when a line wouldn't let go. Sometimes a snagged or fouled line needs to be cut immediately. Leatherman-type tools are the best; I keep a couple just to hand out to my delivery crews. Knives are also excellent for prying off reluctant twist-off beer bottle tops, opening fuel and water accesses when the proper tool can't be found, cleaning fish, and paring apples while on watch.

- A wetsuit, to be used when your prop picks up a line or your anchor becomes inextricably snagged.

- An Emergency Position Indicating Radio Beacon (EPIRB). Every boat that ventures offshore should carry one. The latest model, and most recommended, is the 406 EPIRB, so named because of its transmitting frequency (406.025 MHz). When activated the 406 EPIRB is able to identify itself and transmit to dedicated satellites the vessel's position. Because the 406 EPIRB can identify itself, those who purchase it are required to register it (details upon purchase) and update the registration annually.

- A currently inspected and up-to-date life raft. My thumbnail research tells me that many skippers don't buy one because "they're too bulky and difficult to stow considering the low odds that you might have to use it." Like car accidents, most boating mishaps happen close to home, and whether you're 1 or 100 miles offshore, a properly deployed raft is a life-saver. As far as bulk and stowage, the Florida-based Winslow Life Raft Company will custom fold a soft-pack (vacuum-packed for longer time between repacking) life raft to fit the dimensions that you provide them. You'll be shocked at how compact they can fold the thing.

- Duct tape (last but so far from least!). Its myriad uses need no explanation. Keep at least two rolls available of the good American-made stuff. Some of the foreign knock-offs deteriorate while on the shelf.

Prep the Boat

I always get a kick out of photos of the interiors of large yachts that appear in ads and articles in slick boating magazines. I'm baffled by the freestanding chairs, sofas, and coffee tables; huge, flat-screen televisions just sitting there on sideboards; and hanging chandeliers. I can't figure out how these boats handle rough weather. Even acknowledging that the owners never go offshore, and that the purpose of this kind of boat is dockside "ostentaining"—oops, I mean entertaining—I still can't help thinking that it just isn't shipshape. I wonder how the paid crew gets these boats from Côte d'Azure to Miami Beach with the chandelier intact. Maybe they take it down and air-ship it to the destination? And how about the furniture? Duct tape?

However they handle gear and provisions on the megayachts, it surely involves some level of preparation, and that applies to more modest craft as well. In our world, however, not seeing to the proper stowage of gear and the preparation of our yachts for an offshore jaunt can result in more than mere inconvenience. A near worst-case scenario—and one that is invariably the result of faulty preparation—is engine failure due to clogged fuel filters because of the disturbance of debris in the bottom of the tanks. This usually occurs after encountering turbulent waters. If your boat's primary service has been in protected waters, then a commercial fuel "scrubbing" and tank cleaning should be considered before venturing offshore. But don't stop there. Extra filters, belts, impellers, and other spare parts should be noted and stowed separately from other gear and provisions taken aboard (which should also be categorized and stowed for access when needed). Then make sure that the crew knows where everything is.

Imagine the boat on its side or upside down and then go through the boat and visualize what would happen to all stowed material if that were to occur. After you look at the galley-ware, batteries, tools, personal gear, cleaning equipment, and so on, stow it all so that it will stay in place if the boat undergoes extreme motion. One way to keep it all in place is to make sure that all lockers, cabinets, and drawers have positive locks that cannot open accidentally.

Information In, Information Out

Before you leave the dock, you should both gather and disseminate information. For the "input," most boaters routinely tune in to the current NOAA VHF forecast; however, if the trip will stretch offshore or be of any duration, the NOAA website www.ndbc.noaa.gov offers more detailed forecasts and weather discussions. A relatively recent addition is its "dial-a-buoy" program where real-time sea conditions can be downloaded—or accessed by telephone—from NOAA weather buoys. The website www.ndbc.noaa.gov/dial.shtml explains the system, which can be invaluable prior to immediate departure.

The "output" aspect of disseminating information is a float plan, indicating where you're going and when so that if you don't arrive and can't communicate someone will know you're in trouble and will initiate a search. Although it can be as simple as leaving written word of your schedule with friends, family, or the home marina, the ideal float plan is as detailed as possible and includes the following information:

- Crew list
- Boat's registration and/or documentation numbers
- Course and planned itinerary
- Phone numbers of the marinas that you're planning to visit and your ETAs (estimated times of arrival)

The U.S. Coast Guard offers a plan that you can download at www.floatplancentral.org/download/USCGFloatPlan.pdf, but I find the following format on page 54 to be just as useful and a bit more user-friendly.

Whoever ashore is holding your float plan should be given some idea as to its flexibility. You don't want them calling the Coast Guard just because you got a late start one morning or spent a few hours longer than planned on a passage. Give them a clear idea as to your plans to stay in contact and how much leeway to allow in that plan before taking action. And make sure you let them know about any changes in crew or itinerary during the voyage.

Thunderstorms and Squalls

We had left Marathon's Boot Key Harbor in the Florida Keys late in the afternoon of a muggy April day for the run across the Gulf of Mexico to San Carlos Bay on Florida's west coast. The plan was to be up the Caloosahatchee River in time for breakfast in Ft. Myers's restored downtown. The passage of about 125 miles at a fuel-saving 10 knots would be a delightful full-moon overnighter with a convivial crew, new autopilot, and reasonable weather report.

Stu's Quick 'n' Easy Float Plan

THIS FLOAT PLAN should be filed with an individual or entity (a marina, for instance) known to all persons aboard. It should be updated and communicated daily to that party until the end of the voyage. If any person aboard has a medical condition or a need for medication that can be a cause of concern in the event of delay or accident, that information should be communicated to the holder of the float plan as a separate attachment.

Float Plan Holder (individual or entity): Sam Smith, Phone: 000/555-1212

Vessel Name: Tall Tales

Vessel Description: Trawler, 35-foot, white hull

Life Raft Aboard (Yes/No): Yes

Outstanding Features: Blue bimini top
Inflatable dinghy stowed aft outboard obscuring name on transom

Vessel Details: Builder/type: Monk trawler, 1965
Power: Single Ford/Lehman diesel, 120 hp
Documentation #52361 /State Registration: NJ 63024

People on Board (POB):

Captain	John Jones, Age 57, Cell: 917/555-1212
	Contact: Selena Jones, Phone: 212/555-1212
Crew	Joe Doe, Age 55, Cell: 212/333-1212
	Contact: Serena Doe, Phone: 212/537-1509
Crew	Jane Doe, Age 22, Cell: None
	Contact: John Fawn, Phone: 908/775-2639

(Include sex and age of children, nature of disability of handicapped people, and special medical requirements, e.g., medications, allergies, diabetes, etc.)

Planned Itinerary As of (Start Date): 03/08/09

Departure Point: Ft. Rachel Marina, Mystic, CT, Phone: 000/555-3333

Final Destination and Planned Arrival Date (approximate hour of arrival if applicable, or if voyage is not overnight): City Marina, Charleston, SC, Phone: 000/432-1111, 03/09/09

Destinations

Day One (date) _____: State Marina, Atlantic City, NJ, (phone #)

Day Two (date) _____: Viking Marina, Ocean City, MD, (phone #)

(etc.)

(If Estimated Time of Arrival is after business hours at a particular marina, indicate so and communicate information to holder of float plan.)

That forecast had me a bit concerned, though. A weak cold front was due to reach the area late the next day and cold fronts often usher thunderstorms ahead of them. In my experience, there's no such thing as a weak thunderstorm. But, I figured we would easily beat out the front. OK, so I was wrong.

We lost that gorgeous moon to a heavy overcast about two hours after last light and the western sky (hint: thunderstorms will almost always approach from the western quadrant) lit up with a spectacular display of air-to-air lightning. When we heard the first rumbles of thunder, I decided it was time to go into full T-storm mode. By the time we had entered San Carlos Bay, we had been battered by no less than a half dozen thunderstorms, including one beast that hit us with 40-knot winds, a smattering of hail, and a torrential downpour. We were tired and had spent a sleepless night, but we never considered ourselves in danger.

The classic summer squall usually occurs in the late afternoon of a muggy, high-humidity day. The variations in temperature between the hot surface air and the cooler upper atmosphere contribute to the anvil-shaped thunderheads that can erupt so spectacularly. Squalls not associated with thunderstorms are usually experienced in near-coastal waters or in the open ocean in the southern North Atlantic, Gulf Stream, Caribbean, and Pacific waters. These squalls typically ride the prevailing winds. In the daytime you can spot these "line squalls," so called because there are often two, three, or more in a well-defined row. The line of distinction between the squall and the surrounding waters is usually clear and a planing hull can easily maneuver around them.

After dark, approaching line squalls make a distinctive radar target—they remind me of a horde of angry bees moving across the screen. Most radars target them best on the 3- to 5-mile ranges. In the absence of radar, an alert crew on an otherwise clear night will note nearby stars appear to extinguish as they are overshadowed by the storm's approach. These squalls will often carry rain and may or may not bring high winds with them.

The first step to preparing for thunderstorms and squalls is to be aware. Here are a couple of factors that can add up to trouble: It is late afternoon of a hot, muggy day, with haziness to the west. (Inland and on near-coastal waters on the Eastern seaboard, I've never seen a thunderstorm approach from anywhere other than on a westerly—such as northwest or southwest—component. West of the Rockies, thunderstorms can approach from an easterly or westerly component. Offshore, squalls will come from the direction of the prevailing wind.) Sure, we all know about the anvil-shaped cloud that gets taller and taller as the day goes on. That's a classic indication of trouble, and of course it's a dead giveaway. But often, you'll never see that anvil; the sky will get hazier and darker and the storm could be on you.

If it looks like you are going to get hit by a thunderstorm, you'll know it by an abrupt drop in temperature and, often, a dramatic change in wind direction. During our trip across the Gulf, a 10- to 15-knot southerly abruptly became a 20- to 25-knot northeasterly.

Do not try to run from a squall once it's upon you. Run with the storm and you prolong the time you are in it. Instead, let it pass by and you'll be done with it faster. Aside from very small craft that can get flipped over by the wind, most boats that come to grief in squalls and thunderstorms do so because they tried to take some kind of evasive action and grounded, broached, or were broadsided by wind and/or sea.

It's unlikely that you will experience high seas, but the wind velocity can increase dramatically. In any case, by the time this occurs, it's too late to outrun the storm, so don't waste time trying. Instead, make your storm plans and use what time you have to prepare the boat and the crew, using these steps:

- Keep your radio on. Both NOAA and the Coast Guard will often broadcast an alarm preceded by a tone on Channel 16.

- Begin a careful radar watch. Squalls and thunderstorms are easy to track on radar, and you can gauge their speed, direction, and mass. Often, if there is sea room, you can avoid them or even maneuver between them.

- If there is an option between upper and lower stations, button up the upper station and move below. Don't hang out in the flybridge; the more weight higher up, the less stable the boat will be.

- Use your electronics. Some skippers are nervous about electronics, and we've all heard of lightning strikes that scorch the systems. I believe that my aids to navigation are to be used, and when the visibility approaches nil in squalls and thunderstorms, that's when I want them most. In all the years that I've been doing this stuff—much of it in Florida, the lightning strike capital of the world—I've never been aboard a boat that's been hit by lightning although I've chatted with plenty of people who have, and on more than a few occasions I've seen lightning strike the sea from 30 yards to a half mile away when my boat was the only one in sight. I believe a properly grounded boat has about as much chance of being struck as the adjacent waters. Also, if lightning does strike, it will probably burn your electronics whether you're using them or not. On that note, I always carry a spare handheld VHF and GPS so if the big strike happens I'll most likely still have navigation and communication.

- Drop anchor, if you're able to do so. Get as much scope out as you can, and power into the wind, just enough to take strain off the anchor line.

- If it's not practical to anchor, get the bow into the wind, or just a little bit off of it. Hold it there with just enough power to maintain steerageway and keep the boat stationary.

- Remember that if you're in a relatively confined body of water—like New Jersey's Barnegat Bay; the Chesapeake Bay and its tributaries; Long Island Sound; Florida's Biscayne Bay; the inland bays of the Great Lakes; and the western lakes—it's important to attempt to maintain the boat's position until the squall passes and not allow it to be driven off course and possibly into danger.

When You're About to Get Hit

In spite of prudent voyage planning and a close eye on the weather map, a storm is coming your way and you can't avoid it. You've got a few minutes before things get bad. Let's get to work preparing for it:

1. When observing a buildup of clouds like this, the possibility of a thunderhead—and consequent thunderstorm forming—must be considered. 2. Often, thunderheads build over land prior to moving offshore. 3. A typical anvil-shaped formation is beginning to take shape. 4. Although this well-defined anvil-shaped cloud formation may or may not develop into a thunderstorm, it's best to keep a "weather" eye on it.

- Stow all loose deck gear such as fenders, boathooks, buckets, and personal items below.

- If it's possible to get canvas, such as biminis and suncovers, stowed *securely*, do that. If you don't think the canvas can be secured safely, maybe it's better to leave it in place as wildly flailing, unsecured canvas can be a danger in itself. Roll up and secure the flaps of fully enclosed flybridges so the wind can blow through, rather than allow the enclosure to increase the boat's windage.

- Either remove and stow bow-mounted anchors below in such a way that they can be quickly remounted, or tie additional lines to multiple secure points (cleats, anchor windlass base) to ensure that the anchor does not break loose or swing against the hull, possibly causing damage.

This is a typical squall line formation.

These fenders and all loose gear should be stowed below in the event of inclement weather.

No matter how well secured on deck, this inflatable dinghy will either break loose or contribute toward destabilizing the boat when the wind and seas make up.

- Ensure operation of automatic bilge pumps, and check on the availability of manual bilge pumps.
- Deflate deck-stowed inflatable dinghies to the extent that they can be stowed below. Try to avoid deflating them all the way as they might need to be re-inflated if the boat founders or the life raft does not inflate.
- Tie with multiple lines to secure points deck-mounted recreational floatable gear—kayaks, canoes—that cannot be stowed. However, such large items are difficult to secure properly and can break loose in extreme conditions, possibly putting the mother ship in danger. In that event, plans should be made to cut lashings at key points so that the kayak or canoe can be quickly slid overboard.
- Secure all ports and hatches.
- Close seacocks other than engine cooling and drain and necessary pump valves.
- Rig safety lines if there will be a need for any on-deck activity. Run continuous lines, docklines, spare anchor rode, etc., around the boat, securing the lines at well-backed permanent points such as cleats, windlass bases, and flybridge supports. Deck stanchions are usually not well backed enough or strong enough to be utilized. Care must be taken that excess line is secured and cannot be washed overboard to foul the props.
- Prepare to deploy drogues or sea anchors.
- Explain to all aboard the location and use of life jackets and personal flotation devices (PFDs).

- Assign various crewmembers specific responsibilities, including maintaining a look-out for other vessels, land, and breakers; assuring that PFDs are worn properly by all aboard; maintaining radio watch; maintaining engine watch; seeing that provisions are available to all; and checking bilges.
- Keep snacks, food, and water near. If possible, the crew should eat a substantial meal before encountering storm conditions.
- Encourage those who feel a need for them to take seasickness remedies that will not impair function.
- Communicate the vessel's position to a shore-side party, the Coast Guard, or nearby vessels with a Sécurité call as follows: "Sécurité, Sécurité, Sécurité. This is the motor vessel (describe boat); we are a white, 35-foot express cruiser at (broadcast exact location in latitude/longitude) 27°30' N latitude and 83°55' W longitude. We are presently hove-to and expect to be (or are) restricted in our ability to maneuver due to a (or an approaching) thunderstorm. Any concerned traffic please respond." If another vessel does respond due to relative closeness—and therefore might be experiencing the same weather and the difficulties you're preparing for—and there is some concern of collision, arrange with him to monitor a channel to enable vessel-to-vessel communication for as long as necessary.

When It's Rough

The same sea state will appear differently when viewed from the deck of a 19-foot center console as opposed to the flybridge of a 50-foot sportfisherman. The point at which seas are considered "rough"—for the purpose of definition let's call it a state where some action needs to be taken based on the surrounding conditions—boils down to two general factors: (1) what a vessel's crew observes and (2) the effect on the boat of a particular sea state.

Often, the two are not directly correlated. For example, the crews of two identical boats, one running downwind/-sea and one running upwind/-sea, will experience similar sight pictures, but the boats will react differently. In such a situation, the crew of the upwind/-sea boat will experience violent motion and pounding and consider the conditions "rough" long before their downwind/-sea counterparts. Similarly, crews of larger boats operating from enclosed cabins and sealed flybridges will not be aware of changing conditions as quickly as crews of more exposed vessels.

Changing Sea Conditions

Except in the case of fast-moving fronts or squalls, sea conditions rarely change rapidly; usually changes will be relatively gradual. The observant boater will note an increase in whitecaps, from the occasional wave to groupings of two, three, or more, until the surrounding waters are flecked with whitecaps as the wind increases.

As a rule of thumb, if winds and seas begin to rise on clear cloudless days, the conditions will continue to worsen. Atlantic coastal cruisers then should be particularly aware of the location of the Gulf Stream and stay well inshore of it. The north-flowing Gulf Stream in opposition to a northerly breeze can create dangerous conditions in the form of steep waves. Cruisers off the U.S. West Coast—California, Washington, and Oregon—should be aware that onshore winds of long duration can create large, breaking seas due to the *fetch* (the distance free of obstructions over which the wind has an opportunity to work on the surface of the water) of the Pacific waves. Boaters on inland bodies of water, such as the Great Lakes, need be aware of the short, sharp, potentially boat-damaging seas—the chop—produced by strong winds over these relatively shallow bodies of water.

In relatively small craft—cruisers of up to about 40 feet in length—as surrounding seas increase, the immediate horizon will seem closer. When running in the troughs of building seas, nearby waves will appear to grow from below eye level to "shoulder" height and continue to rise.

As seas rise, larger craft in following seas will begin to fishtail—in other words, the stern will swerve back and forth. This is an indicator that the vessel is traveling at an unsafe speed for the conditions. Running into building seas, bow plumes will increase, heavier spray will find its way aboard, and foredecks will be awash more frequently. All powerboats encountering head seas will experience heavier pounding and will often feel a "shuddering" effect as the boat leaps from the crest of a sea into the trough.

ROUGH WEATHER BOAT HANDLING

While your choice of rough weather tactics will depend upon many variables (including the boat's capabilities, your own skill, the conditions, and the staunchness of your crew), the direction that you're heading relative to the conditions establishes the context for your decision-making. As already discussed, there are big differences when running with the weather, taking it more or less on the beam, or heading into it. We'll look at each scenario separately.

Operating in Following Seas

Most powerboats running downwind/-sea have a tendency to fishtail—for their stern to be pushed around by the waves. If left uncontrolled, a fishtail can turn into a *broach*, in which the boat is forced sideways to the seas and which can result in swamping or even rolling on its beam ends. In worse conditions, with higher, steeper waves, there is also a danger of *pitchpoling*—an end-over-end capsize.

The difficulty of maintaining control in following seas imposes more work and greater vigilance on the part of the helmsperson. Under extreme conditions or after an extended period, the possibility of a mistake due to exhaustion or a lapse of attention increases, so the decision to run downwind/-sea should be made with careful consideration. Another factor to consider is whether there is another crewmember available and competent to take the helm *before* you become exhausted. All that said, running downwind/-sea can, at times, be the right decision, not least because the motion is easier on the crew and the boat than when bashing into waves.

A vessel running at a slower speed than the following seas will find itself rising to the seas as they pass under the boat and then sliding into the trough as the sea continues on its way. As the seas increase, the precipitous rise and then dip into the trough can appear alarming to the crew of a small craft, but as long as the seas are not breaking, little water will come aboard and the craft will not be in danger.

With three not-unlikely hazards awaiting boats overtaking following seas, the importance of reducing boat speed to less than that of the wave progression cannot be overemphasized. Those three hazards are:

1. The boat can pitchpole, as mentioned already.
2. The boat can be "pooped"—i.e., a following sea can break over the transom, swamping the aft cockpit of the entire boat if it's an open one.
3. The boat can slide precipitously down the face of a sea, risking a broach.

Often, the first indication of excessive speed in following seas is the sensation of the vessel "teetering" on the crest of a sea for an instant. The boat will seem to keep pace with the sea on its crest before sliding down the face or the backside of the sea. At that point the boat is not answering its helm well, primarily because the bow or stern might be momentarily out of water. It is important then, to reduce speed gradually until the boat is safely rising to the passing seas as they continue on their way.

Different vessels will react differently in inclement conditions, with the smallest being the most affected. Outboard-powered and stern-drive vessels are at a disadvantage in high seas due to the higher probability of their props cavitating—biting air instead of water as their sterns rise to the seas. The resultant loss of applied power can also lead to a loss of steering control as the props serve as the rudders for these boats. Skippers of outboard-powered and stern-drive vessels, therefore, need to reduce speed and trim their lower units to the maximum down position. The deeper-biting props of most V-drive and straight-shafted inboard cruisers are less likely to cavitate; however, they, too, are best served by reducing speed.

Weight distribution, especially with smaller outboards, including center consoles and runabouts, also becomes more critical. Due to engine, fuel, and battery placement, most smaller vessels carry their weight considerably aft of amidships. The addition of gear and passengers aft can lower the boat's freeboard—that part of the hull above the waterline—to unsafe levels, possibly allowing a following sea to enter the boat or, in a worst-case scenario, to swamp the boat from astern. Therefore, in most circumstances, the less weight aft the better. If practical, aft-seated passengers and gear stowed aft should be moved amidships or forward.

Maintaining Progress

While reducing speed is the prime requisite for all boats when following seas build, you still want to make port in the shortest possible time. Do so by taking advantage of the regular size and spacing of seas that usually prevails offshore. (Seas closer inshore tend to become confused and irregular due to shoaling and variances in bottom contour.)

When running offshore, therefore, place yourself on the back slope of an advancing wave and adjust your speed to that of the wave. As long as surrounding seas are not breaking, such a move can allow for a quicker, yet still safe, trip. Be particularly alert to the conditions all around, constantly adjusting the throttle to keep the boat from overtaking the wave, and steering so as to remain stern to the seas. If the boat outpaces the wave and the seas are not particularly large, chances are you won't pitchpole, but the boat will tend to surf down the face of the wave—once it reaches the trough, the bow will tend to dig in at the same time that the face of the wave continues pushing the stern forward. With the bow somewhat immobilized, the stern may slew around, which can lead to a broach.

Changing Course

A disadvantage of "riding a wave" in this manner is that it restricts your ability change course, since it is so important, especially with smaller boats and larger seas, to keep the seas directly abaft the stern. When it does become necessary to change course, back off until the speed is reduced to where the boat is traveling slower than the following seas. Then observe the "set sequence" of the waves as follows:

- Offshore seas often run in "sets"—for example, two, three, or four regularly spaced seas followed by a gap where the trough between the seas is considerably wider than the trough between the preceding seas. It's in this trough where the course change is safest.

- When the decision to change course is made, speed is reduced until the boat is in the trough between the waves. The boat then proceeds in the trough perpendicular to the seas.

- The distance run in the trough is determined by the height and speed of the following seas. Before the next sea comes on and catches you broadside, turn again to resume course and present your stern to the following sea, placing yourself on its back slope.

- If the necessary course change is a major one—more than a few degrees—and considering the short time the boat is able to remain in the trough, the change in direction can be incremental in nature—a few degrees at a time until the next opportune wave sequence occurs.

Operating in Cross Seas

Do not run in cross seas if:

- The boat appears to "wobble" along the crest of the sea as it passes beneath the hull, and the skipper feels that an abrupt movement of the helm will send it careening off course.

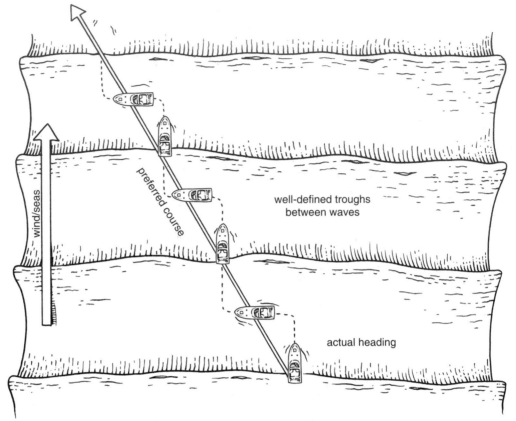

wind/seas

preferred course

well-defined troughs
between waves

actual heading

When traveling in the same direction as heavy seas, it's critical to keep your stern square to the direction the waves are traveling. If your course isn't directly downwind or downsea, make incremental moves in the troughs and square up again before the next wave comes on, allowing it to pass under you.

- The crew has the feeling that the boat can slide down the front or backside of the sea with a loss of control.
- At the top of the crest, the sea appears higher than the surrounding seas and the slide into the trough is swift.

Many deep-V hulls with fore-and-aft chines tend to "lean" into the wind when they are running crosswind or cross seas while on plane. This can lead to a broach or loss of control if the boat is traveling too fast or if there is a sudden increase in wind velocity such as with a gust. If the boat exhibits such behavior or if the crew is uncomfortable running crosswind and cross sea, the preferred course needs to be gained by incremental course changes as discussed in the next section.

If the seas aren't particularly large, however, the boat may continue on a cross-sea course if that's the preferred direction. However, even when it's possible to run safely in crosswinds and cross seas, it can be extremely uncomfortable due to the rolling of the boat as well as the possibility of gear breaking loose and injury to the crew. It might be more comfortable, therefore, to take the seas somewhat forward of the beam with frequent minor course changes to maintain the preferred track.

Operating in Head Seas

The skipper of the boat pounding into head seas learns quickly that it is tough on vessel and crew. The defining term here is *pounding*. Different hull designs react differently to encounters with head seas. For instance a deep-V hull is designed to "slice" through seas and will do so long after moderate-V designs or vessels with a less deadrise aft begin pounding in similar situations. As seas continue to rise, however, even deep-V hulls will reach a point where they begin to pound.

When a vessel begins pounding—that distinctive sound when it slams off one wave and then slams into the next one—not only is it running inefficiently, the strain on boat, gear, and crew increases the possibility of damage, gear failure, and/or injury.

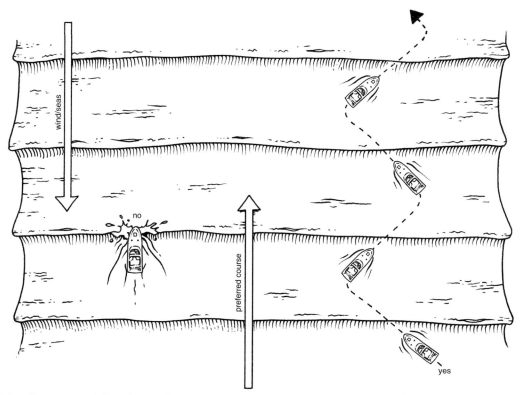

Traveling at speed directly into heavy seas (left) is damaging to both boat and crew. Instead, zigzag toward your destination (right), cutting the waves at an angle and changing directions in the troughs.

Deadrise

A DEEP- OR MODERATE-V hull is defined by its deadrise—the angle of the bottom from the horizontal at the stern. A flat-bottomed boat, by definition, has no deadrise. In a moderate-V hull, the transom deadrise is somewhat less than 20 degrees from the horizontal. There is no hard-and-fast line between a moderate-V design and a deep-V, but most authorities agree that a transom deadrise greater than 21 degrees constitutes a deep-V hull. It's highly unusual to see a transom deadrise in excess of 25 degrees. Technically, the angle at the bow is also "deadrise," but generally it is referred to as the *entry*. Most boats are, of course, much sharper at the bow than the stern. The angle of the hull's bottom decreases from the entry at the bow to the stern. Different designers make this transition in different ways—some more gradually, and others quite quickly—along with a multitude of other distinctions in hull shape that affect boat performance.

Here is a study in contrasting boat designs. The moderate-V hull on *Mari K 3* shows substantial deadrise (i.e., "rise of floor"). *Otter* has virtually no deadrise at the transom.

As seas rise, the boater who continues to take them bow-on will have to slow down to reduce pounding considerably sooner than the boater who takes the seas somewhat at an angle to the bow—how much of an angle will be determined by the size of the seas, the boat's design and speed, and the preferred course. If the course line is directly upwind and sea, taking the seas at any angle other than head-on will be off course. Naturally, the skipper will wish to adhere as close as possible to the course line and still have a comfortable trip. It will not take much trial and error before he determines which approach angle and speed are most efficient and comfortable. Once that combination is found, constant attention to the throttle(s) will save time and make for a smoother trip.

Generally, it's more efficient to apply power as the oncoming sea is approached than to back off as the boat slides into the trough and heads for the next one. Skippers of twin-engined cruisers should ensure that the rpm is the same for both engines by constantly referring to the tachometers. Not doing so could create an unwanted angle to the seas and possibly increase pounding. It will definitely create unnerving vibration, especially as the boat rises to the crest. Vessels equipped with throttle synchronizers have an advantage here.

Incremental course changes are best made in the troughs allowing the boat to "zigzag" toward its destination. Deciding when to make those course changes is easier when the seas are observed for a while and the "set sequence" is determined, as discussed previously.

If, depending on the size, condition of the vessel, and morale of the crew, it appears dangerous to continue into head seas, other options must be considered. Head seas are becoming dangerous when a combination of the following is observed:

- The seas increase in size; more seas are crested with whitecaps.
- It is almost impossible to progress without pounding.
- The boat appears to "climb" the seas at a greater angle, and it appears to "teeter" at the crest before sliding into the trough.
- The boat "surfs" down the backside of the sea before rising to the next one.
- The wind appears diminished in the trough, but more spray is coming aboard.
- The propellers begin to cavitate on the crests.
- The helm appears lighter at times, and there is a delay in response to moving the wheel.
- The crew feels that the boat is in danger, sensing the possibility of capsize.

When It Gets *Really* Bad

When conditions are really bad, the first and simplest step is to stop the boat by putting the bow into the seas and applying just enough power to hold position. Allow the boat to rise to the seas and slide into the trough without attempting to make forward way. The boat should not experience the previously mentioned teetering and steep approaches to the seas, and it should ride relatively comfortably.

At this point, when the decision has been made to stop and not complete the planned trip, it can be considered as verging on a survival situation, and it would be prudent to inform others—the Coast Guard, a commercial towing service, nearby vessels—of your position and situation. While not a Mayday scenario, a Sécurité call, as discussed above, is appropriate. (See When You're About to Get Hit on pages 56–60.)

If the seas continue to rise even farther, the boat will again begin to feel uncontrollable even though it is hove-to, and it takes more power to maintain position. As the seas become steeper, the boat will rise at a steeper angle, and it becomes harder to hold the bow into the seas. The next step is to deploy a sea anchor or drogue as discussed in the next section. You might also reach this decision if the crew becomes exhausted, or if your fuel is running low and remaining supplies won't permit you to continue heading into the seas at the same throttle setting.

Which Way to Head in Rough Seas

BEFORE YOU DO ANYTHING else when encountering rough seas, back off the throttles, whether you're going into the seas or running with them, and take time to think things out.

When heading upwind in deteriorating conditions, putting the bow into the seas at the slowest speed that you can make forward progress is the safest route. Maintaining bare steerageway is especially important in a smaller boat. As long as you're making progress toward your destination, you'll get there safely if you overcome the urge to firewall the throttles. In rotten weather offshore, speed kills as quickly as it will on an interstate highway.

The same holds true for the vessel running downwind in big seas. Overcome the urge to power up. Chances are you won't get in trouble as long as you're going slower than the seas. Let them pass underneath and continue on their way—and in most circumstances that'll work right into an inlet. Sure, you can keep speed up and ride the back of a wave right into the inlet, but if it were to break suddenly or slow down rapidly, which it might as the water shoals, you can find yourself on the crest or sliding down the front and risk going end to end. (See Chapter 4 for more on running inlets.)

It's best in many instances not to take seas head-on. For instance, when the seas are spaced relatively far apart and not too steep, taking them at an angle somewhat off the bow, especially in a smaller boat, will allow you to keep your speed up rather than approach the near dead stop each time you take a wave bow-square. Also, if the destination is not dead upwind, you can make incremental course changes by letting a sea pass under the boat and then running a short distance in the trough and taking the next sea on, or just off, the nose.

DROGUES AND SEA ANCHORS

Drogues and sea anchors are for use in survival situations—when you temporarily give up all hope of going anywhere in particular and your sole remaining objective is to keep the boat right-side up on the water's surface, with all crew inside. Both are trailed or streamed in the water on a line, but they work at opposite ends of the boat. Sea anchors are trailed from the bow, and their primary purpose is to hold the bow into the seas while the boat drifts slowly astern. The drogue is deployed aft. It is designed to keep the stern to the seas and to reduce the boat's speed as it drifts downwind/-sea, running slowly ahead of the weather.

A sea anchor cannot perform as a drogue and vice versa. A drogue is designed to slow the boat down, not hold it into the seas and stop it, which is what the sea anchor is designed for. Therefore, the drogue is typically much smaller than the sea anchor.

The typical powerboater—including canyon runners, long-legged cruisers, and any vessel that dashes out of an inlet—is more likely to encounter the kind of foul weather that can call for some sort of streaming device than the far-ranging sailor who, while he might be offshore for weeks at a time, chooses his season and route so life-threatening

A sea anchor holds this boat securely in place. (Para-Tech)

Sea anchors deploy off the bow to keep the bow into the wind and slow drift to leeward. This commercially available package comes with complete instructions, all set up and ready for instant deployment and easy retrieval. (Para-Tech)

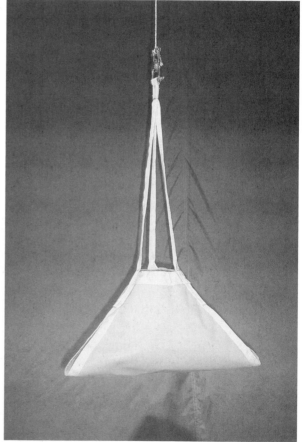

Drogues deploy off the stern to keep the boat from broaching when moving downwind in rough seas. This model comes with all the necessary gear for instant deployment and retrieval. (Para-Tech)

conditions are unusual. Indeed, half a century ago, before our era of instant communication and reasonably accurate weather pictures, it was the rare swordfish or tuna fisherman, long-liner, or dragger who didn't have both a sea anchor and drogue gear stashed below. And even in today's modern fishery, many commercial vessels are so equipped.

The greatest danger in severe seas is of the boat being broached, and then swamped or capsized. The worst position for a powerboat in those conditions, therefore, is to lie broadside to the seas. However, most powerboats will naturally lay broadside to the seas when the engines fail, and every attempt must be made to present either the bow or stern to the seas.

Theoretically, the deployment of a sea anchor will present the bow to the seas while a drogue will present the stern to the seas. The choice of utilizing a drogue or sea anchor should depend on the boat's destination and the possible existence of dangers to leeward. If the destination is to leeward, the deployment of the drogue will allow the boat to drift downwind in the intended direction. If the destination is to windward, the deployment of the sea anchor will reduce the boat's downwind drift.

In my experience, though, I've found that more often than not the deployment of a drogue from a power vessel without power is ineffective. The boat will continue to lay beam-to the seas, and the drogue will stream out to leeward. In contrast, most powerboats will lay bow-to the seas behind a substantial and properly deployed sea anchor. The added advantage of the sea anchor is that the drift astern will be slower, keeping the boat closer to the reported position of the engine failure.

Using Drogues

For the drogue to be effective, power must be available to keep the bow downwind/-sea. The advantage of a drogue on a powerboat is to assist in keeping the stern to the seas, especially in extreme conditions. Properly used, the drogue can slow the boat down, increase stability, and reduce the chances of broaching while you continue on your down-weather course. Utilizing a drogue, therefore, is a sensible option when running downwind in heavy seas. In such conditions, the boat—even under reduced power—can be forced to a speed greater than the seas, thus inviting broaching or pitchpoling. Streaming a drogue will slow the boat down as well as allow the vessel to steer somewhat across the seas with less of a chance of taking green water aboard. If it is absolutely necessary to enter an inlet with a strong onshore wind and breaking seas, that drogue could make the difference between coming in keel-down or keel-up.

It's particularly important that the strain of the drogue be distributed across as wide an area as possible with the use of a bridle. Here's how to rig it:

- Run a nylon line of the largest diameter that can wrap and hitch around the midships and aft cleats. Leave enough slack in the line between the two aft cleats to clear any obstructions such as outboard engines.
- Use a nylon drogue line at least three to five times the overall length of the boat. The line is coiled aft, enabling it to be deployed without snarling.

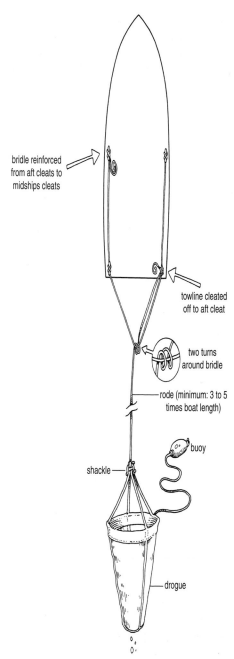

bridle reinforced
from aft cleats to
midships cleats

towline cleated
off to aft cleat

two turns
around bridle

rode (minimum: 3 to 5
times boat length)

buoy

shackle

drogue

To rig a drogue, start with a bridle made of nylon line of the largest diameter that can wrap and hitch around the midships and aft cleats. Leave enough slack to clear obstructions such as outboard engines. Two turns of the drogue line are wrapped around the bridle and then led to one of the aft cleats. The other end is bent or shackled to the drogue.

- Wrap two turns of the inboard end of the drogue line around the center of the bridle. The line is then led around either one of the aft cleats. The outboard end of the line is bent or shackled to the drogue.

- Ease the drogue overboard, and pay out the rode as the boat proceeds downwind.

- Ease out enough rode—at least two or three boat lengths—until the boat and the drogue are "in synch," that is, both in troughs or cresting waves at the same time. The drogue line is eased out around the cleat. Once a sufficient amount of line is deployed, the line is hitched to the cleat and the strain of the rode will be centered at the bridle.

- Place chafing gear wherever the bridle or rode line passes over a solid surface.

Using Sea Anchors

The sea anchor is often called the parachute anchor because early commercial devices were military-surplus parachutes and the modern ones are based on that principle. It is deployed from the bow similar to traditional ground tackle. The proper sea anchor must be powerful enough to hold the bow into the seas without allowing it to fall off so as to lie broadside to the seas.

Sea anchors do not need to be used only as an emergency last resort. Even when severe weather isn't an issue, the powerboater who experiences engine failure can lie comfortably to a sea anchor, thus enabling him to affect repairs or await rescue, rather than rolling in the trough, which is uncomfortable and can be dangerous. I was once caught offshore with a dead engine in conditions so rough that I was barely able to stay aboard, much less work in the bilges, due to the boat's heavy rolling. After deploying a jury-rigged sea anchor, I was able to work below for 5 hours, long enough to make repairs.

But wait . . . there are more benefits. You can rig a sea anchor on a wholly voluntary basis, if you just wish to fish or rest awhile. And in the case of a dead engine, the sea anchor will help hold the boat closer to its last reported position, thus enhancing rescue efforts.

While sea anchor rigging and deployment procedures vary somewhat by manufacturer, here are the basics:

- All deck hardware such as cleats and/or samson posts must have suitable backing plates. If you are not sure the bow cleats can take the strain of a sea anchor, the strain must be distributed to as many points as possible. The most efficient way to do that is to join the boat's bow and midships cleats by a continuous nylon line of the maximum diameter that can be wrapped around the cleats. The sea anchor rode will be shackled to this line at the boat's stem.

- The sea anchor rode must be nylon (for its ability to stretch and absorb shock) and as long as practical, ideally at least ten times the boat's overall length. Both ends of the rode should incorporate thimbled eyes through which shackles can be placed.

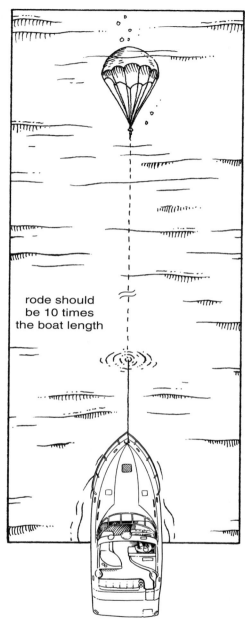

rode should
be 10 times
the boat length

A sea anchor is deployed from the bow when you're in survival mode and have given up trying to achieve forward motion. Initially let out just two to three boat lengths of rode, and then ease out more until a comfortable riding position is found. It's easy to let out more but nearly impossible to bring it in until conditions ease.

- All loose components should be secured to prevent them from being swept overboard prematurely while you rig the device. Coil the rode so it will feed overboard without tangling. This is best done by coiling it on deck or below and then bringing it forward in the coiled position. If the rode was previously coiled for stowage and there is any doubt that it will deploy smoothly, then it should be unwrapped and re-coiled properly.
- The boat should be headed into the seas until all way is lost; secure the rudder amidships.
- The sea anchor is then tossed overboard. A float line and trip line, which are used to facilitate the retrieval of the sea anchor afterward, are usually included in commercial packages; these are tossed overboard at the same time. The sea anchor and gear must be deployed from the windward side of the bow.
- The rode is fed out as the boat drifts astern.
- Once the rode is deployed, set chafing gear—rags taped over the line, even multiple wraps of duct tape will do—where the rode rides over the bow. Inspect the attachment points along the cleats and provide chafe protection where needed.

Once the boat's bow is held into the wind, the motion—and most of the danger—is eased and the crew can rest below until the weather subsides. The downside is that the strain on the gear and boat—especially the stern due to the aft drift—can be considerable. Swim platforms can be trashed, poorly secured or designed transom doors may stove in, and if the rudders aren't exactly centered, they too, can sustain damage.

Equipping Yourself

Determining whether to carry a commercial sea anchor or drogue is up to the individual skipper who has to take into consideration cost, space, and boat use. However, to my knowledge, there is no commercially available combination unit that performs both functions.

Commercially available sea anchors include the Para-Tech, the Shewmon, and the Seagrabber; all basically work on the parachute principle. They are deployed from the boat's bow and are equipped with retrieval lines that allow them to be collapsed so they can be hauled back aboard without encountering excessive water resistance.

Commercially available drogues include the Delta drogue, the Seabrake drogue, the Galerider drogue, and the Series drogue. Para-Tech also manufactures drogue devices.

The basic principle behind these devices is fairly simple, however, so if you're not equipped with a commercial drag device and you find yourself in a situation where you really need one, jury-rigging one is a viable option.

Jury-Rigging a Sea Anchor

The secret to effectively jury-rigging a sea anchor is length of line and the resistance of the material used. The goal is to keep the bow into the seas while minimizing the drift aft and preventing the boat from falling off to leeward. As a rule, the smaller vessel stands a better chance of laying to a jury-rigged sea anchor as it takes less material in the water to bring the bow into the seas. The line is of a length and deployed as discussed in the section on sea anchors above. What is at the end of that long line—usually the anchor rode is utilized—needs to be partially submerged, yet still able to float. There have been a number of instances where a bimini top has been successfully converted to a sea anchor by crossing paddles or boathooks (or a combination of both) across the top and lashing them in place. Bunk cushions with their underlying boards have also been used. It's important to pierce the cushions and the boards and tie the securing lines through them rather than just wrapping the lines around them.

Depending on the size of the boat, the needed weight can be the length of chain at the bitter end of the anchor rode, or the anchor itself (or a smaller lunch hook) wrapped around a number of life preservers.

Most jury-rigged sea anchors fail because the rode and the material used for the anchor part company. Every attempt must be made to ensure a good attachment for the rode. If a bimini is used, the rode should be wrapped around the paddles or boathooks where they cross. A small anchor, diving weights, or the aforementioned chain lead secured to the bimini frame can serve as the needed weight.

Jury-Rigging a Drogue

The jury-rigged drogue stands a much better chance of working as intended than the sea anchor. It doesn't take much effort, a touch of rudder to keep a powerboat headed down-sea. The purpose of the drogue is to slow the boat down to a safe enough speed to allow the seas to pass under it, but not to stop it. Essentially anything streamed aft will slow the boat to some degree.

As stated before, most commercial devices cannot serve as both a drogue and sea anchor. A parachute sea anchor, for instance, if built strong enough to take the strain of trapping the enormous amount of water created by the tow of the boat, can stop the boat completely, thus leaving it susceptible to being swamped by following seas. However, much of the same material, found aboard and mentioned in the sea anchor discussion, utilized differently can serve as a drogue. The anchor rode serves well when unbent from the anchor and both ends secured to the aft cleats or the bridle. Almost anything that creates resistance, such as life preservers, fenders, or bunk cushions, can be bent to the rode. Large items like the bimini most likely will not serve as an effective drogue as they will break, tear, or become detached from the strain of the boat running down-sea. A galvanized bucket well secured and streamed aft can serve as an effective drogue for the smaller powerboat. There have been instances of larger powerboats using water-filled inflatable dinghies as drogues in severe conditions. The resistance of an inflatable in such a case can be intense. The towing line is best when it encircles the dingy or has a number of attachment points and the painter that leads to the mother ship should be secured to a bridle or via a Y attachment, with the strain shared between the two aft cleats.

4
Running Inlets Safely

AFTER 30 YEARS OF RUNNING vessels ranging from three-masted schooners to paddle-wheel steamboats (really!) and just about everything in-between, I figure that I have more sea time than most, and maybe (hopefully?) another 30 years of dining out on the stories I've accumulated. But when I was going over some of my old logs recently, they documented that while most of that time was off-soundings, the stuff of the tales—the hair-raising close calls and life and death scenarios—hardly ever occurred far at sea. No, indeed. They occurred near shore, too darn near for the most part, closing with the coast, transiting from soundings to the deep, and, especially, shooting inlets.

More boaters get in trouble coming in than going out of inlets than probably any-where else, and you don't have to be a rocket scientist to figure out why. The lure of home and hearth causes caution to be abandoned just when it should be grasped ever more tightly. Since more problems occur when coming in, and because circumstances almost never require you to go *out* an inlet in poor conditions, the discussion in this chapter will assume you're on your way in.

When approaching an inlet, I think of it as the beginning of a journey, not the end, even if I'm coming in. Somewhere during that approach, I prepare the boat as I would when getting ready for a storm—not a bad analogy as the conditions inside an inlet can be radically different from what you experience offshore. The gear is secured against everything up to and including a full broach (which happened once, propelling a full dive tank into a running genset, with the consequent short circuit, fire, and explosion briefly convincing me that New Jersey's Manasquan Inlet had been mined). This is the time to do a final engine check and to make sure that lifesaving equipment is at hand and the VHF

Before Approaching an Inlet

TAKE THESE STEPS as you get ready to come into an inlet:

- Do your homework. Be fairly sure of your ETA and study the wind and tide picture. Knowing in advance the time of your arrival, which allows you to be aware of the tidal picture, lessens the possibility of unpleasant surprises. If, upon checking the tide charts, you find that delaying your arrival (or, conversely, upping the rpm to get you to the sea buoy faster) will allow you to take advantage of a friendlier tide—a flood with an onshore breeze, for instance—that entrance can be less stressful.

- Examine the chart carefully for rapid changes in depth. A 30-foot sounding affords plenty of depth for your cruiser, but if that spot is surrounded by areas of greater depth—40, 50, or 60 feet—it can be a candidate for dangerous breakers when the wind pipes up.

- Make sure your filters and water separators are clean and clear. Inlet turbulence will do the Maytag thing with your fuel, possibly stirring up sediment that might clog your filters or injectors at the worst possible time.

- Secure loose gear, especially lines. Fenders shouldn't be deployed until you're inside and in smooth water.

- Determine if there is a Coast Guard unit or commercial tower present. Give them a call if you have any concerns regarding the inlet conditions; they'll be glad to advise and it's free.

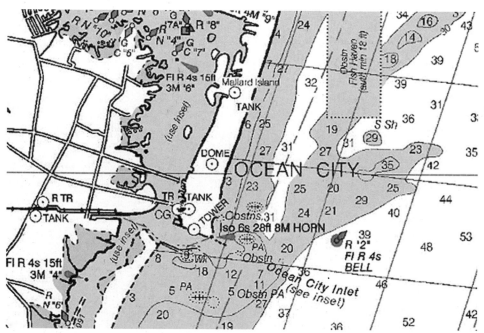

This inlet offers an excellent reason to head out to the sea buoy (R "2" FL R 4s) before setting course toward your next destination. Note the shallower areas surrounded by relatively deep water outside and especially south of the inlet—a birthing ground for breakers in any kind of unsettled weather. (NOAA)

radio is tuned to Channel 16. A particular quirk of mine is to see that everybody is on deck and not below, especially if the entrance is at night or in adverse conditions. Under those circumstances, especially if the inlet is a busy one, I'll broadcast a Sécurité call (see Chapter 3) on Channels 13 and 16 just to let the world know I'm there.

Besides taking pains to ascertain what traffic is about, know the tidal situation. Sure, an adverse tide won't faze most powerboats, but if a fast ebb through an inlet is facing a stiff onshore breeze, it can build up a nasty chop. Add an onshore near-gale to that ebb and you can have breakers across the mouth of the inlet—a fine indication that this is not a good time to attempt an entrance.

It would be nice to say that when conditions are nasty, go elsewhere, but often, we don't have that choice. For reasons of fuel or weather, we may *need* to get in. Keep in mind, though, that conditions will often change with the tide, and it can be only a matter of hours (six at most) before the tide will change and possibly ease your entrance. An ebbing tide, especially when against the onshore wind, will invariably create a nastier scenario than the flood. If you have the luxury of waiting, put your bow into the breeze and hold tight.

Okay, even though the rollers are coming in with the wind clipping their tops off, you don't have the luxury of waiting and you need to come in. Here's where some elements of the deep-V heavy horsepower set believe that putting the pedal to the metal is the way to go. I personally believe that's nonsense and could lead to a loss of control or even, possibly, broaching or pitchpoling. On the other hand, I've never seen or heard of a well-found, well-skippered vessel entering an inlet at a slower speed than the rollers—allowing the seas to overtake and pass the boat—coming to grief: it'll roll and wallow, but it will enter safely.

Then there's the "local knowledge" angle. Many inlets have particular idiosyncrasies that might not show up on the charts or cruising guides but that the locals are aware of. (A good example is a shoal area where breakers can form under certain conditions of wind and tide.) Since the locals have been transiting a particular inlet all their lives, their knowledge can be invaluable. They should be milked for every drop of it, but bear in mind that they haven't been transiting the inlet in *your* boat.

An exception would be if the gale is of such intensity that seas are actually breaking across the inlet. I would definitely not attempt to go in then. If you are not able to wait offshore or go elsewhere, that's the time to holler for help. When the rollers are well spaced and defined, another option is to ride the backside of a sea into the inlet, carefully working the throttles so the boat does not exceed the speed of that sea.

APPROACHING AND ENTERING AN INLET

When approaching a strange inlet and you're unsure of what to expect, it's always a good idea to put out a call on Channel 9 or 16 requesting local knowledge. ("This is *Mom's Mink* approaching Barnegat Inlet requesting information regarding the area; anybody available?") If there is a local tower available, it will probably respond—putting their name out over the airwaves is good advertising—and will be glad to talk you in. On the other hand, beware of the guy who suggests an "easier shortcut" because he's been "running in here all my life" and doesn't mention that he's been doing it in a skiff with an 18-inch draft. Any information you gather should be processed and utilized or discarded as you think best, always remembering that you're the skipper of your boat and the one that's solely responsible for any decisions made.

The name of the game is situational awareness. Before you start the approach, you should have already made yourself aware of the state of the tide, current, and wind as well as familiarized yourself with the layout of the inlet: buoyage, shallows, and such. All of these things should be determined and committed to mind ahead of time so that when you begin the approach, you can devote your attention to the situation as it develops around you and your boat.

Most inlets have a sea buoy seaward of the entrance; that buoy is positioned to facilitate an approach. Identify the buoy on the chart and begin your approach from the buoy. When approaching an unfamiliar inlet—especially in inclement weather—always go out to the buoy first, even when it appears that you can save time by cutting it short. From there:

- Gauge the set of the wind and current while approaching, and make incremental corrections so a major course change at the last minute won't be necessary.

- If there is poor visibility or you're concerned about oncoming traffic, broadcast a Sécurité call on Channels 16 and 13. (See Chapter 3.)

- Don't be so focused on your approach that you're not aware of nearby traffic. Look around—*all* the way around, including behind you. Beware of cowboys coming up the wrong side of the channel toward you or passing you from astern. (Yeah, it's stupid. And yeah, it happens all the time.)

- When faced with an oncoming vessel that appears to be acting inappropriately or dangerously—or one that's crawling up your tailpipe—remember that taking evasive action, or a change in course and speed, should be your absolute *last* option. Use this option only when you truly believe that not doing so will result in a collision. Get on Channel 16—even when you think that the other vessel is not on the air, such as a PWC or a muscle boat—and call the vessel, and then immediately give the PAN-PAN call. (See Chapter 8.) This indicates that you are transmitting an urgent message. When there is no answer you can then transmit the danger signal over the radio and follow it up with the horn. This transmission goes like this: "This is the incoming 35-foot motor vessel *Tall Tales* located between the jetties of the St. John's River Entrance. A 45-foot express-style motor vessel is approaching me from astern at a high rate of speed and has not answered repeated radio calls. I am now transmitting and sounding the danger signal." (Sound five short blasts with your horn.) As soon as possible once you're through the inlet, detail what took place (or almost took place) in your log. The Coast Guard will be listening and, in the event of an incident or inquiry, your actions will be closely scrutinized.

- Don't ease your vigilance once you're into the inlet. What's next? Is a course change necessary or a bridge to call?

APPROACHING INLETS FROM DIFFERENT DIRECTIONS

It's a fairly good bet that as you approach an inlet from offshore, there will be a change in the conditions that you've been experiencing. That can be due to a number of factors, such as a gradually shoaling bottom or the nearness of the land, that have a modifying effect—or sometimes an aggravating effect—on the wind and tide situation. In any case, it's something to be prepared for. If you're been quartering cross seas for hours, for instance, don't expect those conditions to continue right into the inlet. Those seas can rapidly become head or following seas as you near land, and change yet again, as you begin your approach into the inlet.

As already stated, it's a matter of situational awareness. By being aware of the conditions you've been running in, you'll be alert to the nuances that precede a change and better able to avoid unpleasant surprises.

Cross Seas

In cross seas, apply just enough power to overcome the effect of the seas and maintain your course, and quarter them, taking them somewhat aft of the bow. Of course, if you're in a narrow or heavily trafficked channel, you might not have that option. If you're in a small craft and running beam-to the seas might be dangerous, it may be wise to either wait until the conditions change (in tidal areas it probably will change with the change in tide), or wait until the traffic eases before beginning your approach. Whether you decide to wait or come in under cross seas, this is a good time for a Channel 16 Sécurité call.

When making that cross-sea approach, while it may appear that your bow is pointing up-wind and up-sea from the inlet's entrance, the boat's "track," your actual course, should be center channel. Often, you will lose the effect of the quartering wind and seas just as you enter the protected water between the jetties; it is important then not to overshoot—that jetty can get real close, real quick. Be prepared to back off the throttles and gently swing onto a direct course.

Following Seas

When approaching an inlet with a following sea, keep in mind that seas leading away from you can appear smaller than they really are. Stand off a while so you can gauge them. If there's another boat ahead, you'll get a good idea of the size of the seas as it settles into the troughs. If the seas look particularly boisterous, check the tide again. An ebb tide flowing against an onshore breeze will create more of a chop. Maybe it's best to wait for the change of tide when things will likely calm down.

When you do make your approach, throttle back and allow the seas to outpace your boat as you slowly enter the inlet. In larger seas, the rise and fall can appear precipitous as the boat appears to ride the crest and slide into the trough, but the forward progress will be steady and the boat will be easily controllable.

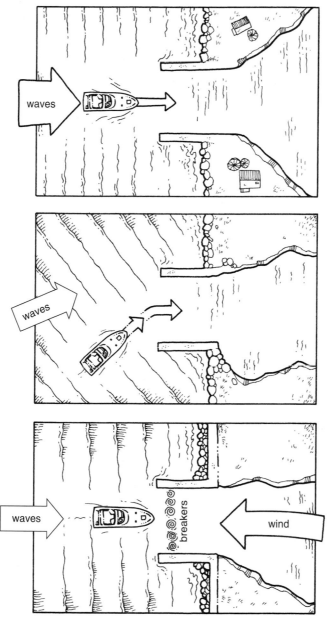

When approaching an inlet with a following sea (top), keep your transom square to the waves. As tangential waves enter an inlet (middle), they'll straighten out, so changing course in the inlet will keep the waves on your transom. Onshore waves and an offshore breeze (bottom) may produce breakers at the mouth of the inlet, in which case, the best approach is to wait for slack water.

If the seas are regularly spaced and entering the inlet is straightforward—not at an angle and not breaking—it may be possible to place the boat upon the backside of the advancing sea and ride it into the inlet. If so, begin the approach by placing the boat on the back side of the wave, at least 10 to 15 boat lengths from the inlet entrance. Determine that the course will lead directly into the inlet without any need for incremental course changes. If it doesn't appear to be a straightforward approach, reduce power and ride in at a slower speed than the seas; doing so will allow safe, incremental course changes.

Once into the inlet, the seas will most likely rapidly diminish or possibly break. Usually there will be smooth or relatively calm water ahead. Being careful to stay in the buoyed channel or as close to the center as possible, increase speed to exit the turbulence quickly and access protected water.

If there is a strong onshore breeze and it becomes difficult to reduce speed enough to safely enter the inlet, larger twin-screw vessels, especially those with relatively wide beams, can have their engines placed in reverse and power slowly increased to further reduce speed. In a smaller single-screw craft, placing the engine in reverse is not a good idea. The power needed to have an effect in reverse will be great, and the torque of the prop in reverse can kick the stern in one direction or the other (to port for boats with right-handed propellers). You'll then try to compensate with the rudder, with the result being highly tenuous and unstable steering in a situation in which you need as much control as possible. Even considering taking such an action in a single-screw boat indicates that the boat is verging on excessive speed in heavy winds and/or seas and that a different approach is required. It is essential that the seas be directly abaft the boat to prevent a broach, and it would be wise to deploy a drogue as discussed in Chapter 3.

Head Seas

Due to the close proximity of land to windward, head seas in an inlet are rarely large. They tend to have a short, sharp chop, which can put additional strain on boats, gear, and crew. Ideally, the best time to make an approach in head seas is during the last hour of the ebb, or slack water preceding the flood. During a flood tide, the seas can be expected to be more turbulent as the tide will be in opposition to the wind.

If the inlet is wide enough and traffic allows, a zigzag approach is best. Instead of taking the seas head-on, take each sea at somewhat of an angle, thus allowing speed to be maintained and avoiding the shock of pounding directly into the sea.

As the seas can rapidly diminish once into the protected waters of the inlet, be careful not to overshoot in one direction or the other, and to remain in center channel.

5

Maintaining Your Poise in Fog and Darkness

It had been a tough run bringing the old sportfisherman down from Miami to Cristobal/Colon in Panama, where the owner was anxiously awaiting his boat. On the last leg, we were running between 10 and 12 knots due to carburetion problems and a dinged prop on the starboard engine. By the time we picked up the lights of the city, it was well after dark. The boat was surfing down 6- to 8-footers driven by a rising northeast wind, and we were darn near exhausted. Not to worry, I told my mate, because there, intermittently flickering above the wave tops, was the flashing breakwater light, just where the GPS said it was supposed to be. I aimed for it thinking of the cold beer and warm sheets just beyond its beckoning flash.

But something didn't seem right, so I hauled myself up the tower to get a good look. That's when I saw the white phosphorescence of breakers directly ahead and to port. Abeam, there were jagged shadows against the dark water, clumps of rocks that we had already passed. I came down off that tower, turned hard to starboard, firewalled the throttles, and sprouted a few new gray hairs. As it turned out, I had been steering for an airport beacon a few miles inland. I had just assumed it was the correct light and never bothered to time it or take a proper bearing.

Having almost dug a new Panama Canal, I can attest to the folly of making assumptions that are not based on solid evidence.

LIMITED-VISIBILITY PROCEDURES

All boaters suffer from impaired vision when night falls or the fog rolls. At these moments, even the saltiest skipper will white-knuckle the wheel. Once you're familiar with a few of the following seamanship skills, which have worked for me over the years, you can cruise with confidence in the dark and murk and reach port safely.

Out Go the Lights

When I know I'll be running after dark, I like to keep the hammer down during daylight hours and then back off for a while when the shadows fall—even if only for a short time. It's an old delivery skipper's trick that eases the transition from good to poor visibility and gives your psyche, and eyes, a chance to adjust. You'll find yourself feeling right at home and you'll soon be powering up again.

Run a darkened ship—no white lights except at the stern, which you shouldn't be able to see anyway. Most instrument lights are red, which is OK since they won't affect your night vision. If a boat's interior lights don't have red filters, keep them off and use a red-lens flashlight below.

Ruined night vision can take long minutes to recover, so use your spotlight as sparingly as possible, and don't wield it like a light saber in a *Star Wars* movie. The flashback from your superstructure will ruin your night vision as well as the vision of anybody it strikes. The same goes for your cockpit floods, which will destroy the night vision of everyone behind you.

If you are trying to pick up the reflective tape on unlit buoys, try a low-powered flashlight before using the mega-light. The only time I use the gazillion-candlepower spotlight on my boat is for a quick flash at a particular buoy. To make sure I don't get blinded from the reflection of the light against my boat's white topsides, I attached a cardboard shirt backing to the underside of the light's lens with duct tape. It acts as a shade.

When running in shallow water during periods of reduced visibility, be aware of areas of phosphorescence surrounded by relatively calm water. The phosphorescence can be

Taping a cardboard deflector to a spotlight will prevent glare from reflecting off surfaces on the boat and into your eyes.

caused by the disturbance of water over a shoal. Other indicators of shoaling are areas that appear "frothier" in comparison to surrounding waters and a sudden closely spaced chop when wind and sea conditions have not changed.

When the Curtain Comes Down

Fog is a different matter than just running in the dark. On a clear night, at least you can still see lit aids to navigation, shoreside lights, and other boats' running lights. And you know (or *should* know) precisely when the sun will rise. In dense fog, sometimes you literally can't see to the end of your foredeck, much less the #5 can that must be *somewhere* around here, or that other boat whose engine sounds WAY too close. And unlike the sun, fog is unpredictable. It probably won't last as long as nighttime darkness, but then again, it might.

Running in thick haze or fog, therefore, requires a different set of skills. It is not a question of making time here; anybody who attempts to get somewhere fast when the murk rolls in is a fool. The Rules of the Road recommend you run at "moderate speed," and court rulings have interpreted that phrase to mean "bare steerageway" when visibility is severely reduced. I have my own rule of thumb: I should be able to bring the boat to a dead stop within my field of visibility. If you're staring at a real pea-souper with zero visibility, for practicality's sake, you should run at a 3- to 5-knot pace with frequent stops.

Those stops are important. Often, due to the vagrant nature of fog, you'll hear the whooshing sound of another boat slicing through the water before you'll hear its engines. It's easiest to hear these sounds when you're away from the sources of noise aboard your own boat. I like to throw the throttles in neutral and, as the boat loses way, wander up to the bow and give a good listen.

I am also meticulous about keeping a log in limited visibility. This might seem archaic, but it has saved my bacon more than once. I note the course and compass bearing every hour. This way, if the electronics decide to go AWOL, I'll always be able to figure out where I am. Of course, at the beginning of each season, I see to the accuracy of that all-important compass.

Radar: The Good and the Bad

I WOULD GUESS that radar has caused just as many collisions as its use has avoided. That's because some boaters put blind trust in this component, and, as a result, they get overconfident and run at high speeds. I've been using various types and models of radar for 30 years and have been more amazed at what it doesn't "see" than what it does. However, a well-tuned set will be a lot more efficient than one that hasn't been tuned correctly, so it's important for you to tune the unit on your boat as specified in the instructions. If you have an auto-tuned set, remember that it will target well in good conditions, but when the seas are up, it may lose poorly reflected targets. In inclement conditions, such as periods of rain or snow, most radars are most effective in the lower ranges. Of course, radar must be utilized in limited visibility, but always as an aid. It should never be your first line of defense.

PREPARING THE BOAT FOR A NIGHT RUN

Every ex-GI recalls, usually not so fondly, stripping and cleaning his weapon blindfolded while a hovering instructor reminded him of the consequences of ill-preparedness. While, hopefully, nobody is planning on taking potshots at us boaters, being able to find gear and operate equipment by touch is not a bad concept when preparing for a night cruise.

I always run a darkened ship at night—running lights and red-tinged instrumentation only—because I fervently believe in maintaining night vision. And I don't want to ruin it all by switching a light on to find something. Before the trip, I try to place whatever I'll need so that I can grab it by touch. I put life jackets, heaving lines, docklines, my tool kit, and first-aid packet where I can lay hands on them sight unseen.

A boat I run has a powerful spotlight mounted on the cabin roof. While the on/off switch is at the helm, its power switch is on the electrical panel—as is the power for the anchor release. Before I wised up, there were times when I needed to get that spot on or the hook down and had to grope around the panel, finally using a night-vision-destroying flashlight to find them. Now I count switches down and can find them blind. After you've firmly remembered the critical switches so that you can activate them without too much thought, you can devote some brainpower to memorizing some of the more mundane ones.

I always turn the pressure pump switch off when running—day or night—because if a hose breaks or a fitting fails, I won't hear the pump cycling itself to death over the noise of the engines. But when passengers want running water, they want it now, so I show them how to find the panel switch by feel when they need to hit the tap. That's a good test. Can you find the important switches on your panel without looking? It can come in very handy some day—or night.

To protect your night vision, learn to locate switches for critical circuits by feel.

Collision Avoidance in Poor Visibility

To avoid collisions when visibility is limited, take these steps:

- As visibility decreases, reduce your speed accordingly.
- Have the VHF radio always tuned to Channel 16. (Channel 13 should also be monitored as commercial traffic will often monitor 13, but not 16.) While most radios have a "scan" or "watch" feature enabling two or more channels to be monitored, skippers of vessels that spend time offshore with the possibility of encountering inclement weather or poor visibility often opt to carry two radios aboard.
- Know your exact position to the tenth of a mile at all times—and be prepared to communicate that position.
- Transmit a Sécurité call when crossing a traffic zone, giving your exact position, boat name, course, and speed. (See Chapter 3.)
- Maintain a regular radar watch. Usually I monitor the 3-mile ring and regularly adjust the range up and down. While every radar is unique, generally they are all more accurate at closer ranges. Remember that the effectiveness of radar diminishes in seas and rain.
- Know the proper sound signals to give (see Sound Signals in Limited Visibility below), and use them as instructed by the Rules of the Road.
- Listen carefully for the sound signals of other vessels. In heavily trafficked areas, it is a good idea to periodically shut down the engines, step outside the pilothouse or helm station, and just listen.

LIGHTS

With rare exceptions, a fixed red, green, or white light—one that isn't flashing, blinking, or revolving—is either on land or attached to another vessel. (There are some exceptions. Specialized vessels, like law enforcement boats, commercial towing services, high-speed ferries, surfaced submarines, and hydrofoils, are required to have rotating or flashing lights. The first in a line of pushed barges is also required to show a flashing amber bow light as well as its red/green running lights.) However, if the light you spot on the horizon blinks or exhibits any type of sequence that can be timed, it most likely is a navigational aid.

If your mind is tired, or you're anxiously looking for a particular light, you can convince yourself that the fixed navigational lights of other vessels—or a lamppost on shore—have the sequence you're expecting. This can be of particular concern when there are intervening seas between the observer and the light being observed. The seas can make the light appear to have a sequence—possibly the one you're looking for. Using a stopwatch to time the light will indicate whether it is an actual sequenced light or not.

Aids to Navigation

Most lit navigational aids exhibit some kind of sequence that can be observed and timed. There are very few lit navigational aids in the United States that exhibit fixed or steady lights. The sequences of lit aids are listed on nautical charts and in the Light Lists. Light Lists are government-issued publications that are easier to read and a useful supplement to the information on nautical charts. (Another particularly useful publication is Chart No. 1, which is a booklet that explains chart symbols and light characteristics.)

Compare the sequence and timing of observed navigational aids with those indicated on your chart. Changes in characteristics of lit buoys—especially those in a long channel leading inshore from a sea buoy—can be significant. For instance, when approaching a channel from seaward at night, it is likely that you will see a series of timed red or green flashing buoys. They will be indicated on the chart as FL G 4s or FL R 2.5s, which means that the light will flash green every 4 seconds or red every 2.5 seconds. Often, however, the chart will indicate QR or QG next to a buoy; that is a "quick-flashing" red or green light, which will flash at least sixty times a minute. Upon examination of the chart, you will notice that the quick-flashing light is bringing attention to a change of some sort, possibly a bend or dogleg in the channel, an obstruction, or a nearby shoal area.

When running a channel, especially in the Intracoastal Waterway (ICW), one strategically placed lit aid will appear as you leave the next, so stay center channel to avoid hitting the unlit aids. In tortuous channels, match the aids with your chart; boaters have gone aground by heading for an aid that's around a bend or twist in the channel. The lit aids in such channels will always have varying sequences. Match the sequences with the chart—a stopwatch helps—and you cannot go wrong.

Harbor and channel lit navigational aids can be obscured by background lights on land that are often considerably brighter than the aids. However, the background lights hardly ever have the kind of sequence that navigational aids do. Slow down and scan the area. Your eyes will pick up the aids and with a little practice you will spot them for the beacons they are.

Lights on Vessels

The range lights of far-off ships can be deceptive when an offshore haze/fog combines with a moonless night. When you see them, figure about half the distance that you would on a clearer evening. Often, there will be a "loom" about a ship's range lights that will make it difficult to distinguish its forward range light from the aft. If you see "haloed" reds or greens—they will appear diffuse in the haze—that ship is very close, and it's time to scoot out of his way or chat with him and let him know you're there, as you can never trust another vessel's radar to spot you.

There are numerous light configurations for various vessels out there, but be intimately and instantly familiar with the basic range and running lights of ships and the towing lights of tugs and barges. In a nutshell, the lower of a ship's two white 225-degree

Lights for Power-Driven Vessels Under Way

starboard side view   bow   stern

Under 164 ft. (50 m), masthead light, sidelights, and sternlight.

Over 164 ft. (50 m).

Lights When Towing

Under 164 ft. (50 m), two white steaming lights and towing light aft (yellow over white).

Vessel being towed shows sidelights and sternlight.

If tow is over 657 ft. (200 m), three steaming lights.

Lights When Pushing

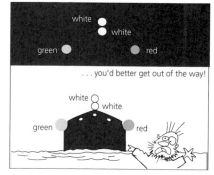

In inland waters only, the lights are as shown, with the yellow bow light flashing. In international waters, there is no yellow bow light, and the two yellow stern lights are replaced by a white stern light.

Deciphering Lights at Night

If you see this at night . . .

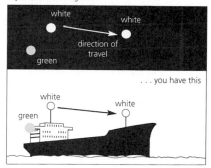

If you see this at night . . .

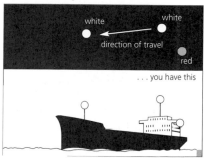

If the two white lights are aligned . . .

Memorize range lights on ships before venturing out at night. (Jim Sollers)

range lights is forward and the higher is aft. Therefore, if you see one above the other in range, the ship is heading directly toward you. The required visible range of a ship's running lights is significantly less than that of his range lights. Therefore, if you observe his red and green as well as his range lights, the ship is probably less than 2 miles away.

Barges have their own light configurations (red and green running, no range lights), but in real life, barge lights are often dim and hard to see. The tug that exhibits three white towing lights is towing his barge(s) astern. The tug that exhibits two white towing lights is either pushing or towing alongside. If you spot a tug with three in-line white towing lights, don't even think of passing astern of it; a towline can be unexpectedly long.

There is hardly any clearance under this closed lift bridge. It must be approached cautiously and plenty of distance off maintained until it's safe to proceed.

The bridge begins to open. An approach must not be attempted until it's all the way up. At night the red light on top of the span will turn to green when it's safe to proceed.

It's safe to proceed, but maybe you should wait until the traffic clears. Then, it might be a good idea to remind the bridge tender that you're still coming through.

Bridges after Dark

Currents around bridges can be deceptive in the dark. A quick, well-aimed burst of your spot at the base of the bridge fendering or an approach buoy will give you a good idea of a current's speed and direction by its apparent "wake."

The navigable span of a fixed bridge will always have a light in its center. Head directly for that light. Two or more bridges parallel to each other—such as multilane highway bridges—will have lights on both navigable spans. Those lights are designed to be used as a range—keep them in line as you pass underneath. This is advisable as bridges rarely cross bodies of water at exact right angles and by keeping the lights in line, you will maintain center channel.

Bascule, lift, and swing bridges will show red lights over the channel when they are in the closed position; green lights will show when they are open for boat traffic. A closed swing bridge will often show what appears to be a triangle of red lights over the channel. As the bridge swings open, two green lights will appear in line signifying that the bridge is open to boat traffic.

On almost all bridges, fixed and movable, there will be wooden fendering around the pilings of the preferred span. Often there will be a fixed red light on the fendering just adjacent to the channel. This light provides another point of reference during your approach as well as delineating the fendering.

Giving way to commercial traffic around bridges is always good policy, but especially so after dark. If in doubt about a vessel's intentions, chat with them. Most monitor VHF Channel 13, which is also the bridge channel everywhere in the United States except Florida, where bridges monitor Channels 9 and 16 (hail on 9).

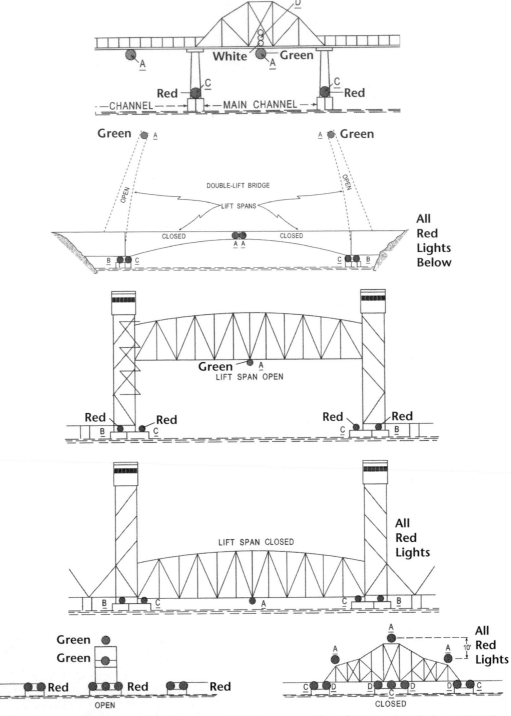

Different types of bridges, and their open or closed status, are identifiable by their lights. (NOAA)

RUNNING RANGES IN LIMITED VISIBILITY

Florida's Anclote River is a shoal-flanked tidal ditch that meanders about 5 miles from its intersection with the Gulf Intracoastal Waterway to the delightful Greek-flavored village of Tarpon Springs. The Anclote is excellently buoyed—necessarily so due to its torturous course. Where the river makes a sharp bend to the north about a mile or so before its terminus off Tarpon Springs' famous sponge docks, a pair of range markers helps boaters negotiate the turn—most boaters, that is. Periodically, when the lust for Greek cuisine overcomes my innate caution, I negotiate the Anclote and there, right off that buoyed and ranged bend, all too often, sits a forlorn cruiser, high and dry on the flats waiting for the next tide. Fortunately, due to the mucky bottom and the required slow speed, damage is usually restricted to the skipper's ego. But the sight of a stranded boat being guarded like a lonely sentinel by the landward range marker, itself high and dry, isn't restricted to the Anclote; I've seen it wherever ranges rule, which encompasses many miles of the ICW.

As far as I can determine, most of those boaters bit the mud because they couldn't figure out when to quit the range. They discovered the hard way that range markers aren't buoys. They headed for the markers on the assumption that the range kept them in good water so far, therefore, it must be safe to carry on a bit farther. As a matter of fact, many range markers are in shoals or on dry land. While a careful study of the chart will indicate when to pick up a range—there will usually be a dotted line connecting the ranges and the light characteristics differ from the surrounding buoys—knowing when to leave it may not be as clear cut.

In some places it's easier to determine ranges. In some western rivers, the southern reaches of Florida's St. John's River, North Carolina's Cape Fear River, and sections of the ICW through South Carolina and Georgia, for instance, one range will lead to another. These are no-brainers as you'll jump out of one as the other lines up. In the Anclote, two green markers for the next leg of the channel fall into line and form a range of sorts, and that's the time I change course. In other areas, though, exercise caution. Often, the next buoys in the channel will come into view while you're still in the range; that's not necessarily the time to head for them. A general rule to follow is that the farther the angle is from 90 degrees, the greater the possibility of error. In other words, it's better to move sharply onto a new course than to gradually enter it. I prefer to wait until buoys are abeam and then come hard over.

Running ranges at night is actually easier than negotiating them during the day. The ranges' distinctive light characteristics will always stand out from other buoys or surrounding ambient light. Often, the leading marker will be a quick-flash (QR, QG) that will line up with an isophase (ISO) flash (equal intervals of light and darkness). In some areas, such as New York Harbor's East River Channel, the range lights will appear brighter when you're in the range and will seem to dim when you swing out of it.

When night running and there isn't another actual range to swing into, generally, a lighted buoy will hove into view, which will be your next marker. As in daytime running, the time to change course is when that buoy is directly abeam and not before.

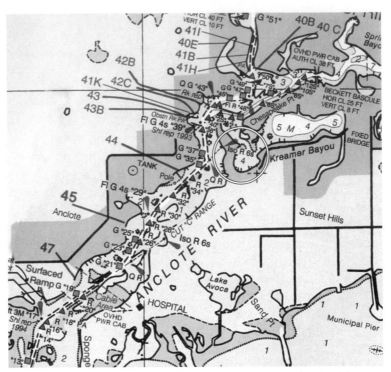

Note how the boater is directed from one range to another in this channel. Changes in channel direction are often indicated by quick-flashing buoys (here QR, for "quick red"). The QR buoys serve here as channel markers as well as being part of the range sequence. Range markers are often located on dry land or atop a shoal (like the ISO R 6s markers circled above), so it's important to study and understand the chart before entering any channel. (NOAA)

An often overlooked and important aspect of any range is the "back bearing." The same range that you followed bow-on, can be utilized stern-to when reversing your course. And ranges don't have to be the charted ones; they can be where you find them. When I'm in a narrow channel, or trying to keep closely to a particular course, I utilize impromptu ranges as aids—a marker that lines up with an object on land or two buoys in line, work just fine.

The bearings we use to determine if we're on a collision course with another vessel are also impromptu ranges. You don't need to use a hand bearing compass or the primary compass to set up a bearing range with an approaching vessel. If it appears that there is any possibility that you're on a collision course, maintain your course and speed and set up a range with the other boat with any part of your vessel that you can eyeball—a stanchion, a windshield post, or an antenna. If that bearing doesn't change significantly and steadily to one side or the other, you are on a collision course. At that point, the Rules of the Road come into play. If you're the burdened vessel, give way. If you're privileged, attempt to communicate with the other vessel. If he doesn't respond or change course or speed and you fear a collision, then the Rules allow you to take whatever action necessary to avoid a collision.

SOUND SIGNALS IN LIMITED VISIBILITY

The Rules mandate certain signals when under way in fog, mist, falling snow, and heavy rainstorms, day or night. Under those circumstances, a power-driven vessel is required to give one prolonged (2-second) blast every 2 minutes.

The danger signal (five short blasts) is also considered a fog signal and is perfectly acceptable to use when you're concerned about collision, even though you cannot see the other vessel. But let's be real—unless equipped with an automatic device, most boaters are erratic in their compliance with the Rules. Note, however, that when you do let loose with a blast and another boater hears it, he'll blast you back. That will make you both more cautious, which is just where you should be.

The more you use signals in fog, the more you'll become aware of the peculiar properties of sound. For instance, with a little practice, you will be able to determine the existence and direction of another object (boat or land) just by listening to your own signal. There will be a slight echo or a change in tone when the blast is bounced off an object. Recently, I noticed a subtle change of tone in my own blasts and barely avoided a drifting sailboat—his white hull and sails perfectly blended in the soup—that was making no signals.

6

Anchoring and Rafting with Assurance

Recently, I oversaw the restoration of a classic 1930s Wheeler motoryacht that had been in my customer's family since the boat was new. I had introduced three generations of heirs and heiresses to boating aboard the old beast and for a good part of that time had been arguing for its restoration. When the work was completed, ten enthusiastic members of the family and I piled aboard for a long weekend at the Hole-in-the-Wall anchorage off Grand Abaco Island in the Bahamas. This was a bunch that disdained marinas and to whom anchoring out was a way of life—an attitude that I helped instill—and, therefore, I paid particular attention to the yacht's ground tackle. A state-of-the-art Italian windlass graced the bow and 300 feet of top-quality stainless steel chain reposed peacefully below.

As we approached the anchorage, the ship's company gathered at the bow to watch this first drop. The skipper, the family's patriarch, tripped the switch from the pilothouse and the anchor let go, followed by the satisfying roar of chain running through the hawse—then silence, deafening silence, as the final link found its way to the bottom. I had neglected to secure the last section of chain. I turned to face the ten questioning—and heretofore, trusting—faces.

"I can't think of a better way to impress upon you," I said loudly, as I retreated below to get my dive gear, "how important it is that one part of the anchor rode be attached to the boat." And I would say, chain-down, that is the most important factor in anchoring, making all else that follows just that.

GROUND TACKLE

How many anchors to carry and of what type is a question that every boater needs to ask. The answers vary according to the boat, its cruising area, and the skipper's preference. For

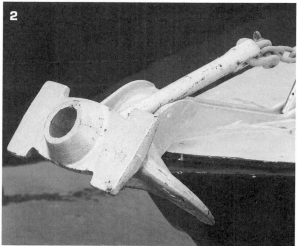

1. Bruce anchor. 2. Rarely seen these days, this old Navy-style anchor depends on "weight of iron" for holding capacity. 3. Danforth anchor. This particular example is not stowed carefully; a wave or wake could knock it overboard. 4. Fluked or plow-type anchor. Note the stainless steel "kick plate" that protects the yacht's topsides. 5. Twin over and under anchors.

starters, though, one anchor is never enough for the obvious reason that it can get lost. The primary anchor always needs a backup *of equal size and function,* although an anchor of a different design might be preferred—a plow-type primary and a Danforth-type backup, for instance. The cautious far-ranging boater also might have a Herreshoff- or yachtsman-type hook stashed in the bilge for emergencies. These anchors are handy for remote eventualities because there are versions that can be broken down or folded for easy stowage.

Each anchor must have its own dedicated rode or anchor line. The amount of rode deployed is known as the scope, and the more scope the better. Scope is determined by the depth of water measured from the vessel's bow chock. A boat anchored in 15 feet of water, with a bow chock 5 feet above the water, would have to let out 60 feet of rode to achieve a scope of three to one: $(15 + 5) \times 3 = 60$.

I won't drop the hook unless I can deploy a minimum scope of 3:1, and that's with heavy tackle and good holding—*and* only if there's no room for more. Ideally, 7:1 should be the minimum, but in the real world of crowded and diminishing anchorages, it's often impossible to get that much rode out without becoming intrusively intimate with your neighbor, who might not be as diligent scope-wise as you are. When circumstances permit, there is no such thing as too much scope. The amount of scope deployed should only be limited by practicality—the amount of rode the boat can carry or the proximity of other anchored vessels.

If space or holding conditions are not ideal and you have to use less scope than you're comfortable with, an intermittent or full-time anchor watch—a crewmember whose primary responsibility is to determine that the anchor is holding properly—needs to be assigned.

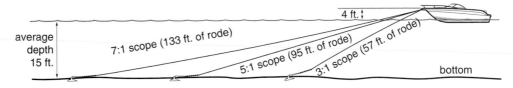

15 ft. of water + 4 ft. of freeboard = 19 ft.
7:1 scope means 7 x 19 = 133 ft. of rode

3:1 scope with chain: pull still nearly horizontal

The longer the scope and the greater the catenary, the more horizontal the pull of the rode on the anchor and the greater the anchor's resistance to pulling out. (Joe Comeau)

The curve of the rode as it arcs up from the anchor to the boat is called the catenary. The catenary is important because the greater the arc, the more line there is lying along the sea bottom, which means that the rode's pull on the anchor is more nearly horizontal. The closer to horizontal the pull, the more the anchor will tend to dig in and maintain its set. Conversely, the more vertical the pull, the greater the likelihood that the anchor will pull out.

Partly for this reason, a rope anchor rode should never be bent directly to the anchor. There should also be at least a fathom (6 feet) of chain between the rope rode and the anchor, and more is better. The chain facilitates the anchor and rode lying in line along the bottom. (Another reason for the chain end on the rode is that it protects the rope from abrading on the bottom.) Why not just carry all chain then? Some larger boats do, but for most vessels it is impractical because of its weight and stowage needs. The nylon anchor rode, due to its elasticity, also serves a shock-absorbing function.

Always secure the bitter end of the rode in the anchor locker (it's *so* embarrassing when that loose end goes overboard). It's important that the end can be released quickly and easily, either to bend on additional line in a strong blow, or in case you need to leave the anchorage instantly. To facilitate this, secure the bitter end to a strong eye in the anchor locker with a quick-release shackle. If it is necessary to abandon the anchor and rode for any reason, the end should be buoyed with a fender or similar object for later retrieval.

Traditionally, anchors have been rated by boat size—the larger the boat, the larger the recommended anchor. In recent years, a number of "lightweight" anchors of different designs have entered the market. These anchors, instead of depending on "weight of iron" for their holding power, depend on their mechanical design to grab the bottom. Some anchors are designed for optimal setting in particular bottoms (grass, rock, coral, shale, etc.), while others are designed to set well in a variety of bottoms. Every year or so, another anchor design comes out that claims to put all the others to shame. The fact that many of the old favorites like the CQR, Danforth, and Bruce, as well as their various spin-offs and knockoffs, are still in use—indeed, that they dominate the market—should make one at least a little bit skeptical about the marketing claims of newcomers.

An inclusive discussion of the various types of anchors is beyond the scope of this book. To find the anchors best suited for a particular boat, a skipper with some knowledge of the particular bottoms where he expects to drop anchor can peruse the extensive literature—complete with suggested anchor and rode charts based on boat size and type—published by every major anchor manufacturer.

Having said that, the anchors that have worked best for me in most bottoms, exclusive of rock, shale, and coral, have been based on the traditional plow (e.g., CQR) and fluke (e.g., Danforth) types. (The Herreshoff- and yachtsman-type anchors are designed for the above-mentioned bottoms.) I've had best results when the anchors were the weight recommended by the manufacturer for whatever boat I was on, or somewhat heavier.

There are "lightweight" versions of the plow- and fluke-style anchors that the manufacturers claim hold just as well as their heavier brethren. I have used these anchors extensively and found that the manufacturers' claims are correct—under normal circumstances. Once the lightweight anchor finds the bottom and sets, it will hold well. However, in extreme conditions—such as in a gale when the boat is being driven quickly astern or when anchoring in cross seas or in a chop amidst fast-moving currents—the lightweight anchors did not perform satisfactorily. They took too long to set, required numerous attempts to set, or, on occasion, didn't set at all. So I admit to being an unreconstructed traditionalist. I believe that the heaviest anchor rated for a particular boat, attached to the maximum diameter nylon rode fronted by at least a few feet of chain, is the way to go.

GOOD TO THE FIRST DROP

Recently, I watched two 35- to 40-foot cruisers leave a perfectly delightful but somewhat tight anchorage because they couldn't set their anchors. They came to a full stop, dropped appropriate hooks, deployed what should have been sufficient scope, backed off, and were surprised that the anchor didn't take.

What went wrong? The two cruisers had committed the most common anchoring error. They dropped their anchors and rodes in massive piles on the bottom. When they backed off, all they did was stretch the rode without setting the hook. The proper procedure is: (1) drop the hook until it hits the bottom and then immediately begin backing to lay the rode with sufficient scope; (2) stop again and then slowly come astern until you feel the anchor take; and (3) come astern harder until you are satisfied that the hook is set correctly. That's it; there are no deep, dark secrets or "Voila" techniques. Follow that procedure and the odds are you'll be securely anchored; well, you should be. Like everything else in this uncertain world, nothing's guaranteed. If it doesn't work and you know you did everything right, just pin the blame elsewhere (like on the crew, which always works for me) and try again.

TO DRAG OR NOT TO DRAG

Once the anchor is set to the skipper's satisfaction and everybody relaxes, it's necessary to determine periodically that the boat remains where it's anchored. How frequently you should check position depends on the holding (i.e., how well your anchor remains embedded in that particular bottom), weather conditions, and anxiety level of the crew. But even under the best of circumstances, checking position should be done with *planned regularity.*

The traditional method is to take the bearing of a fixed object using the primary or a handheld compass. The object is sighted utilizing the lubber line of the compass—if a handheld one, each sighting should be taken from the same position aboard—and the bearing noted. Theoretically, the bearing should remain the same each time the procedure is repeated, thus assuring that the anchor hasn't dragged. In actuality, though, due to the boat's swing, the bearing can appear to change, when, in fact, the anchor isn't dragging. If possible, bearings should be taken of more than one fixed object such as a structure on land and a nearby buoy—although if the buoy is a floating one, it too, might have a certain amount of swing that needs to be taken into consideration. By observation, the swing of the boat will be predictable and bearings can be taken at certain points in the boat's swing of the fixed object. For instance, if the boat's bow is at a certain angle to the object at a particular point in its swing, the bearings taken at that time should be fairly consistent. A few degrees either side of an initial bearing upon successive bearings is not cause for alarm; a consistent change in one direction, however, is a sign of dragging.

Other anchor-watch "modalities" include electronics such as radar and GPS. Some GPS receivers have an "anchor watch" function that can be programmed to sound an alarm when the boat moves a specified distance from the initial position. I would not depend solely on electronics, however, to determine if the anchor is dragging. Supplement them with a visual bearing.

If the anchor does drag, often just deploying more rode, if conditions and room allow, will allow the anchor to reset itself. If that doesn't happen, start the engine, lift the hook, and repeat the whole anchoring procedure while the choice is still yours.

TWO-ANCHOR METHODS

One anchor, well set, will serve most purposes, but there are two scenarios in which setting a second anchor makes sense. The first is for the additional holding that a second anchor affords, as when the boat is anchored in a strong breeze in an area of relatively poor holding, for instance. The other is when the vessel is anchored in an area of swift, reversing tidal currents. In the first case, the anchors are set approximately 45 to 60 degrees apart. In the second, known as a Bahamian moor, the anchors are set about 180 degrees apart.

Knowing when to use the Bahamian moor requires that you understand both the tidal situation and the prevailing winds. The Bahama Islands feature tides that run every which way, depending on the configuration of the channels, while the wind usually blows from the same direction. It is common in many areas for the wind to blow more or less at right angles across the tidal stream. As the tide reverses, the wind will cause the boat to swing in an arc downwind of a straight line drawn between the two hooks. As long as the wind remains from the same direction, the boat will never swing over that line. If the wind reverses direction, however, the boat will swing over the downcurrent rode when the tide reverses, and the props or hull will ride over and possibly foul the line.

The Bahamian moor would seem ideal for a crowded anchorage as the boat—held in place by the two rodes—will swing in its own length. Unfortunately, as you'll be out of synch with the swing of conventionally anchored boats, there is a possibility that there will be bumps in the middle of the night.

Either the mother ship or a dinghy can be used to deploy the second anchor. Whether you're deploying the anchors at 45–60 degrees or at 180 degrees, the procedures are similar.

Using the Mother Ship

When using the mother ship to deploy the second anchor, follow these steps:

1. Set the first anchor. (See panel 1 of the illustration below.)

2. Back off, letting out rode until the boat is situated in the preferred position. Mark the anchor rode at the bow chock with a piece of tape or a small line threaded through its strands.

3. Motor slowly, or drift down if it is downwind or downcurrent, to the area where the second anchor is to be deployed. A crewmember should feed out the anchor line and ensure that it does not become entangled in the prop.

4. Deploy and set the second anchor. The rode is marked as explained above at the bow chock. (See panel 2.)

5. Try this trick if sufficient crew are available: have a deckhand at the bow feeding rode aft to another stationed at the stern, who will ensure that the prop is clear of both anchor lines.

6. Once the second hook is set, take in the rode of the first hook until the previously marked point is reached, whereupon it is belayed to its cleat. The rode of the second hook is then taken in until its previously marked point is reached, and that rode, also, is belayed. (See panel 3.)

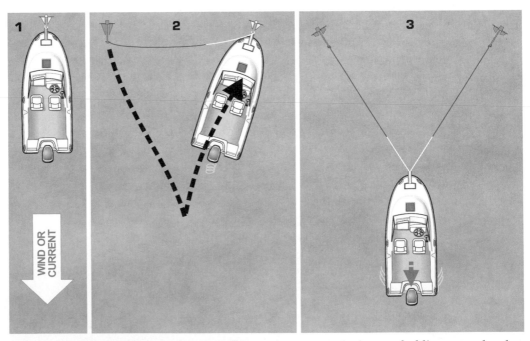

Setting two anchors at 45 to 60 degrees will increase your security in poor holding ground and strong winds. (Bob Sweet)

Using a Dinghy

These are the steps for setting a second anchor using a dinghy:

1. Set the first anchor from the mother ship. Ideally and if circumstances allow, the first anchor should be set upwind or upcurrent from where the second anchor will be deployed.

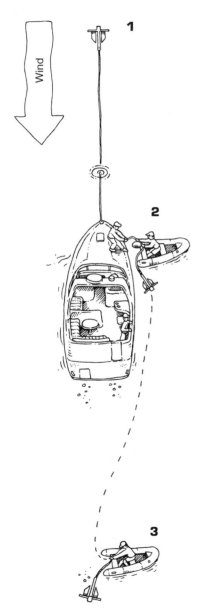

A Bahamian moor allows the boat to swing with changing wind or tides. It can be set from the mother ship in a manner similar to the 45-degree anchoring arrangement shown previously. It can also be set from a dinghy.

2. Launch the dinghy once the first anchor is set and the mother ship is lying in its chosen position.

3. Have another crewmember lower the second anchor by its rode and chain lead until it's hanging next to and outside the dinghy. At this point it would be a good idea to ensure that the end of the rode aboard the mother ship is safely belayed—ideally, to the cleat where it will be tied off when the procedure is completed.

4. Have the dinghy operator secure the anchor to the *outside* of the dinghy using disposable small line—parachute cord is excellent. The anchor should *not* be placed in the dinghy, as the action of deploying it could then destabilize the dinghy. If there is no outboard attached to the dinghy, the anchor can be secured off the dinghy's transom. The line should be wrapped in a number of turns around the anchor and then led inside the dinghy to be tied to seats, thwarts, or other strong points. The means of knotting isn't important as the line will be cut to deploy the anchor. Place the chain lead and a few feet of rode in the dinghy in such a manner that it will not snarl when deployed.

5. If the area of preferred placement of the second anchor is downstream of the mother ship, allow the dinghy to drift down with a crewmember aboard the mother ship feeding out rode. If the preferred area is upstream, the operator rows or slowly motors to the area of deployment while the crewmember feeds out rode. When the preferred area is reached, the operator cuts the line, allowing the anchor to drop without having to lift it over the side of the dinghy.

6. Once the crewmembers and dinghy are back aboard the mother ship, engage the engines and place in gear to set the second anchor. Often, the first anchor line will have to be paid out somewhat and then re-belayed until the second anchor is set. During this procedure, it is important to ensure that all lines are clear of the props.

KEDGING OFF

Kedging is the act of using an anchor so that the boat can be pulled by its rode to another position. Usually a kedge is set to haul a boat off a sandbar or a beach. Kedging can also be utilized to move the boat from one position to another without using the engines, for example, if you're already riding to the hook in an anchorage and you find that you're a little too close to another anchored boat or to a shallow rock. Rather than start up the engine, kedging may be the easiest way to shift the boat a short distance.

The procedure for setting a second anchor with the dinghy is the same as outlined immediately above when it becomes necessary to set an anchor for kedging purposes. When a kedge is set—usually the largest anchor available—the maximum amount of rode and chain lead as practical should be used, as the anchor will be drawn toward the boat before setting.

SPRINGING THE ANCHOR

As any Patrick O'Brian or C. S. Forester fan knows, a prime objective of the skipper of an eighteenth-century warship was to bring its broadside to bear on target—a feat accomplished by adroit handling of the sails when under way. However, often the enemy was land-based, a fort or town, wherein the warship at anchor became a stationary gun platform. Here's where the square-rigged frigate and a modern vessel find common ground—we all lay to wind and tide. There are times, though, when that's just not acceptable. To O'Brian's Captain Aubrey or Forester's Hornblower, lying to an offshore breeze meant he couldn't bring that broadside to bear. And the skipper of today's powerboat can find that lying to his anchor can become downright uncomfortable when he's beam-to an incoming swell in an otherwise snug anchorage.

Aubrey's and Hornblower's answer was to "spring the anchor," hauling their frigates around until their cannon faced the enemy (always the hapless French). We, too, can spring the anchor, thus getting the bow into that rogue swell and allowing an easier ride on the hook.

The trick is to bend a line, nylon preferably, to the anchor rode utilizing a rolling hitch. The spring line doesn't even have to be the same diameter as the rode—the beauty of a rolling hitch is it works with lines of different diameters—although it's best if both lines are the same composition (nylon to nylon, which is what your anchor rode should be anyway). Attach the spring about halfway up the rode between the hook and the stem, run it to the aft cleat on the side that you want the boat to point, and take up on it until your boat swings around and the bow faces into the swell.

Of course, "taking up on it" could be problematic if your boat is of any size and heft or if you're working against a significant sea. Our eighteenth-century heroes had sufficient crew, aft windlasses, and tackles to do the job. Unless you're aboard your megayacht, you probably don't have the same advantages. In that case, you'll want to "sweat" the line. Just take a turn around the cleat until the line is taut; then have a crewmember push

A spring line attached to the anchor rode with a rolling hitch allows you to set the angle of the boat relative to wind or seas for the most comfortable ride.

1. This black stern line is under strain. I want to transfer the strain to the white line so the black one can be removed from the cleat. This calls for a rolling hitch. I prepare to take a turn with the white around the black. 2. There's the first turn (I always use two). The turns go under the standing part of the white line. 3. There's the second turn. Now I'm ready to finish it off with a half hitch. 4. There's the half hitch on top. It's simple. I just wrapped the working end of the white line under itself and tightened it up. I'm holding the end of the white line in my right hand; the part that's going to take the strain is in my left. 5. I pull the white line tight, and it has jammed around the black line and taken the strain, leaving the black line slack. This hitch will hold as long as there is some strain on it. To remove just ease it off and work the knot loose.

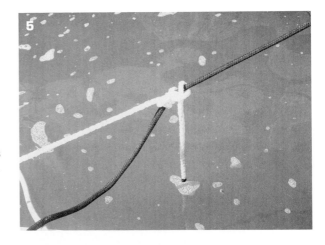

down on the line forward of the cleat until it gives and then let up quickly. As the line goes slack for an instant, take up on it. Keep going until the boat comes around; do it quickly and you'll establish a rhythm with the boat's momentum and it will be that much easier. It works no matter the boat's size; myself and a 110-pound, 5'6" female crewmember once sweated a 90-foot yacht into a 20-knot breeze—and she said she's game to do it again as soon as she recovers. If you have an anchor windlass, you can also lead that spring line around the aft cleat and back to the windlass (after first removing the rode and tying it off to a bow cleat) and then use the windlass to take up on the line. Upon completing this traditional maneuver, you may fire when your guns bear.

RECOVERING A FOULED ANCHOR

The past collides with the present in fascinating ways. My history lesson occurred a few years ago while anchoring in the Thames River off New London, Connecticut, to watch a fireworks display. (This was held to commemorate the burning of the town by the British, who evidently didn't do a very good job as the town still exists.) When I went to hoist the anchor, it refused to budge. I then followed a series of age-old procedures to free a fouled anchor.

First, I brought in line until the rode was "up and down." I took in all the slack and then some, until the bow was somewhat depressed and "rocked" the boat in forward and reverse to force the anchor free. Sometimes, when the rode is tight like that, the wake from a passing boat can also provide the leverage to break it free—sometimes, but not that time.

I then came ahead slowly in the exact reciprocal of the direction in which I set the anchor. This works 90 percent of the time—except in New London that night. I then went off in different directions to the set of the anchor, hoping that would free it. Nope.

As I had experienced fouled anchors in the Thames before, I had buoyed my anchor with a 5/8-inch nylon line (the same diameter as my rode) bent to the crown of the anchor. It is always a good idea to buoy an anchor by this means if you're anchoring in an area where the possibility of fouling exists. In crowded anchorages it also tells others where your anchor lies. I picked up that buoyed line, led it to my windlass, and took up on that—still nothing, which was a first for me.

At that point my guests (it was a charter) indicated that they would really like to go home, so I freed the anchor cable, buoyed it, and departed. The next morning I returned with my dive gear, followed the buoyed rode down, and discovered that my CQR anchor had embedded itself in an old corroded chain with links that were half the size of my 45-pound anchor. After two tanks of air, a dozen hacksaw blades, and a broken pry bar, I freed my hook and brought up a section of chain that turned out to be from a warship circa 1780—those wily Brits.

Unless you're another victim of the Revolution, the points made above should answer for most fouling situations. However, a frequent cause of a foul is when another boater anchors nearby and crosses your rode with his. When it comes time to up anchor, you might bring his hook up with yours. This could be a negotiable situation if the other boater(s) is aboard, but if the other boat is unmanned, the approach needs to be different as casting him loose could create problems. The procedure here is to drop back and feed out enough line until you can pass around the stern of the other boat; then begin taking in the line and you should be clear.

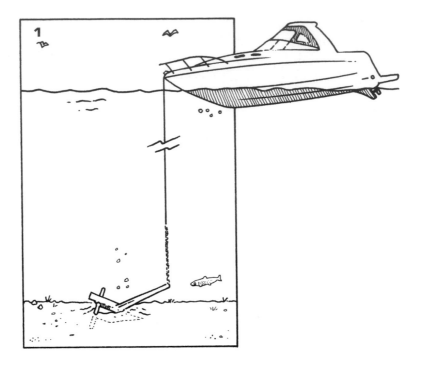

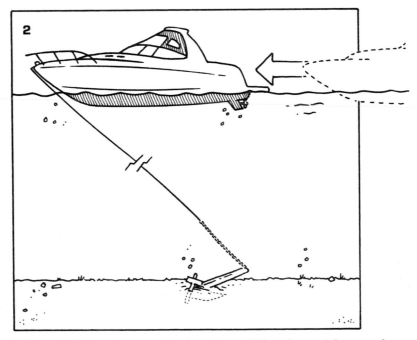

To free a fouled anchor: 1. Bring in rode until it's tight, straight up and down; 2. Drive it out by powering in the direction opposite of which it's set.

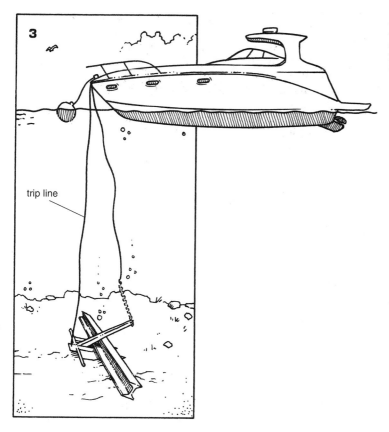

3. If you rigged a trip line to the anchor's crown, haul it in, using the windlass if necessary.

trip line

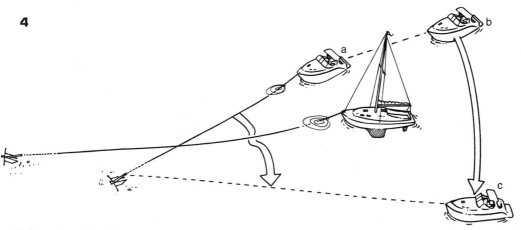

4. If the rode is fouled by another boat's rode, let out enough scope (a) so that you can drop back (b) and pass behind the other boat (c).

DEPLOYING A STERN ANCHOR

It seems that every season in my neck of the woods—Connecticut's Fisher's Island Sound, which is a tidal steeplechase as compared to a tidal race—the local blue-lighters are fishing out some boaters who ended up getting swamped subsequent to anchoring by the stern. Usually it's a couple of fishermen in a small runabout who, for whatever reason, decided to anchor stern-to before dropping a hook. They then discover that the back of the boat reacts somewhat differently than the pointy end when confronted by a few million gallons of fast-moving water. Throw in a wake or a steep chop and it's Swamp City.

I can't think of too many reasons to anchor stern-to, but if I really, really, needed to, I sure wouldn't do it by securing the anchor rode to a stern cleat and dropping the hook. In every one of the half-dozen or so swampings and/or cleat failures that I can recall offhand, the boater had anchored that way, and that was the end that tipped before the big water came in. However, there can be a scenario where you're anchored in a quiet cove and you want the breeze to waft through from stern forward, thus the stern anchor.

In that case, bridle the thing. Run a line to both stern cleats. Tie a bowline knot on the end of the rode, with the loop around the bridle so that it finds the middle. If there were to be anything other than a minimal strain on those cleats, I would back them up by running additional lines to the midships and forward cleats so they will share the load. On the other hand, if there were to be anything other than a minimal strain or anchorage conditions other than a flat calm, I would drop the hook from the bow and seriously consider investing in an air conditioner.

MIDSHIPS ANCHORS

Back when I was delivering expensive boats for very particular clients, I learned an important lesson the hard way. I was tied up alongside a seawall for the evening when some yahoo went by throwing the mother of all wakes. The boat rode up over the fenders and smashed into the wall with caprail, stanchion, and glass damage.

My customer, who was a physician, told me that one of the first things doctors learn in medical school is: if you can't help your patient, at least don't make him worse. In my case, this translated as: if you're going to tool around in other people's boats for a living—don't break them. Then, to add insult to injury, this doctor, who was also an experienced boater, asked me why I didn't spring the boat with a midships anchor to keep it off the wall. Good point. This technique can prevent serious damage to a vessel that needs to be tied up to an exposed dock or seawall for any period of time and where the possibility of damaging wave or wake action exists.

When making your approach to the dock, drop the hook from the bow as far off the dock as practical—at least one or two boat lengths—amidships of where the boat will be when it's secured. Just feed out the line and don't attempt to set the anchor until you're tied up.

Once the boat is secured to the dock, tie a line to the outboard stern cleat and lead it forward to the center of the boat. Bring the slack anchor rode aft, and place a loop (bowline) in that stern line around the anchor rode. Take up on the anchor rode and the pull will be transmitted through the midships bowline at the center of the boat and the boat will be sprung off

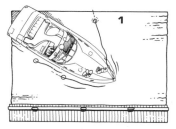 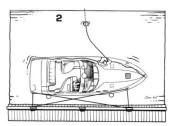 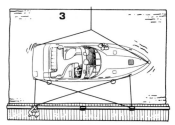

Setting a midships anchor. A properly placed midships anchor can keep your boat from slamming into the dock in poor conditions. Approach the dock slowly, and when one or two boat lengths off, deploy the anchor and feed the rode out but do not set it (panel 1). Keeping the anchor line slack but being careful to avoid prop entanglement, berth and secure the boat as you normally would. Then run another line from an aft cleat to approximately midships. Lead the anchor line aft to midships and bend the two lines together with a rolling hitch (panel 2). Take up on both lines until the boat is safely off the dock. Secure the anchor line to its cleat forward and the aft spring to its cleat aft (panel 3). It's a good idea to buoy a midships anchor beforehand. A small fender will work. Write "anchor" on the buoy with waterproof marker and keep an eye on it to foil fender-gatherers.

the dock. It doesn't have to be far—enough so that the fenders are a couple of inches clear. If a wash comes in, the fendered boat will still ride against the dock, but the anchor spring will stretch, pull it off, and attenuate the hit enough, usually, to prevent damage.

If you need to set an anchor after the boat is tied up, row or motor the anchor out with the dinghy. Sling the anchor and its chain lead on the transom, *outside* the dinghy, holding it in place with a length of inexpensive line tied off to a thwart. Have your crew feed the rope rode to you from the mother ship as you row or motor out. When you get to where you wish to drop the anchor, just cut the line.

Either way you set the midships anchor, it's a good idea to buoy it with a small fender, tying a line somewhat longer than the water depth to the anchor's crown. That will warn passing traffic that there is an anchor below.

ANCHORING FROM THE TOWING EYE

Chafing of the anchor rode probably accounts for more lost anchors than any other cause. Most chafe occurs where the rode passes over the bow chock or anchor roller. The probability of chafe increases when anchored in a rambunctious anchorage—when beset by extreme tidal changes or incoming swells or seas. But if your boat is equipped with a well-backed towing eye at the stem, you can virtually eliminate the chafe to the rode. Anchoring to the towing eye also lowers the point of attachment on the boat, which reduces the angle of the rode and thus increases your holding power for any given length of rode, or allows you to set out less rode for equal holding power. Here's the drill:

- Deploy and set the anchor.
- Fasten a nylon line to the towing eye with a bowline or a shackle. The line should be at least the same diameter as the anchor rode and twice as long as the height from the

Towing eye. In order to use a towing eye as an attachment point for the anchor rode, the eye must be well-backed with plates of a solid material such as stainless steel or aluminum.

waterline to the towing eye. Depending on the size of the boat and the amount of bow overhang, you might be able to do this from the deck, possibly with the help of a boathook, or you might need to get into the dinghy.

- Using a rolling hitch, bend the other end of the line to a point on the anchor rode somewhat forward of the stem towing eye.

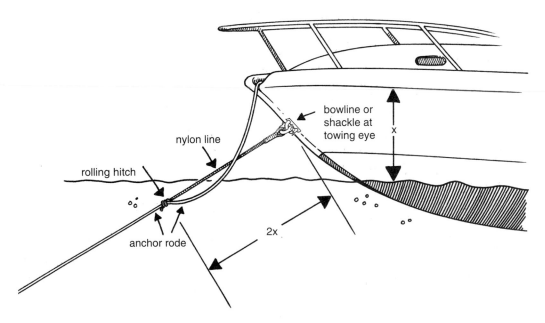

Anchoring by the towing eye eliminates chafe to the rode at the bow chock and lowers the angle of pull on the anchor.

- Let out more anchor rode until the strain is taken by the new line. The original rode will become slack as the strain is transferred.

- Secure the original rode to its cleat. In the event that the rolling hitch does not hold, the strain will be transferred back to its original attachment.

RAFTING

I'm sure that somewhere in *Guinness World Records* is the World's Largest Raft-Up. It probably took place on an obscure lake in the Midwest, where gigantic weekend raft-ups are as popular as hockey brawls in Montreal. Coast Guard search and rescue missions have reportedly taken place wholly within the confines of raft-ups. Rafting, however, is part of boating and, as such, needs to be performed safely and with the proper protocol.

- The largest boat in the raft sets its largest anchor. All of the other boats depend on that anchor, and all will swing as one.

- Like any large family, the littlest tykes are at the edges—the smallest boats should be the outermost, sizes descending from the largest out.

- Outlying boats do not set anchors even when the raft will not be swinging as they won't ride to wake and swell in synchrony with the boats lying alongside.

- Fendering is the key to happy rafting—especially when the owner alongside is a mite quirky about his brightwork. Here's where fenderboards come into their own— especially if each of two boats tied alongside has its own board out, properly adjusted to compensate for differences in topside heights. The trick is to adjust the height of the fenders to match those of the vessel alongside and then lower the board so it matches up with the board of the adjoining boat. However, even if one boat doesn't have a fenderboard and the other does, properly spaced fenders will keep the hulls/board from contact. It's important when using a fenderboard to ensure that fenders are hung within a foot of the ends of the board to keep the board from pivoting in and dinging the boat.

- The lines between boats need to compensate for horizontal as well as vertical movement; therefore, the lines should always be angled fore and aft—spring lines—then taken up snug. Nylon is better than Dacron as it has more give. Lines that run directly across (breast lines) are not a good idea as they can put a strain on the cleats when the boats move in opposite directions.

- If you invite sailboats into your raft, it is best that they not raft alongside each other, as a good wake or roll can slam their spreaders together and get them all tangled up in each other's shrouds. Put powerboats between them (this will also expose the sailors to an alternative lifestyle). If they insist on rafting alongside each other, stagger them so that their masts aren't directly opposite. This applies to powerboats with tuna towers and outriggers also.

I think the world's record is a 200-boat raft-up. Go for it.

7
Towing Without Tension

This chapter goes into some detail about proper towing procedures, especially how to secure lines to both the towing vessel and the vessel under tow in order to lessen the possibilities of mishap or damage to either. "But sometimes, ya gotta be practical." That's a quote from Larry, the owner of the small Brooklyn, New York, boatyard that I worked in as a teenager.

We had received a call from a customer whose cruiser had run aground off Staten Island. Glancing at the tide chart, Larry immediately dispatched me with the yard's work launch. Upon arriving, I saw that the situation was, literally, precipitous. The yacht had run aground on a sloping sandbank, but as the tide receded, that slope became the edge of a cliff that the yacht was teetering on. Its exposed props and shafts—which we had recently installed—were suspended inches above a jagged, rusted mass of steel that appeared to be the boiler of an old wreck.

I got a line across but then became bogged down trying to yell directions to the yacht's crew on how to properly get tied off. I was concerned that the pull from my boat would put an undue strain on his bow cleat, so I wanted to make sure that he had a proper towing bridle rigged. Meanwhile, the ever-receding tide was preparing to drag the yacht into the rusty maws of destruction. In the midst of the yelling back and forth, Larry roared up in another boat. Within seconds, a line shot from Larry's boat to the yacht, and I heard his stentorian bellow to the crew "just wrap it around the cleat and stand back," while he stood at the stern making a figure-eight motion with his fist. They got the idea quickly as Larry belayed the other end of the line to a stern cleat on his boat and then firewalled the engines.

He did everything wrong. The yacht's cleat almost pulled clear off the deck, and Larry's boat skidded dangerously as it took the uneven strain of the tow. But the yacht found deep water, and it was a lot less expensive to replace the bow cleat than the shafts and props. The moral of this story, of course, is that it's important to know the right way to do things, but sometimes, ya gotta be practical.

A popular sight in any busy boating area is the flashing yellow light of a commercial tower—pros like Sea Tow and Towboat U.S.—hauling a disabled vessel back to the dock. At first glance that line-astern tow looks easy, but of course we weren't out there, possibly battling wind and sea, when the tower was hooking up. Also, take a look at the tower's gear: a sturdy deck post centered aft, with carefully coiled loops of nylon line of various sizes nearby, and a made-up bridle ready to be passed to the downed boat is stashed below—not to mention the wealth of training and experience aboard. Combined, all that can help take the snags out of a tough job.

But hang out offshore often enough and that job can fall to one of us—members of the great majority of boaters who aren't towing professionals. It's a big ocean and it's not hard to imagine situations where you're the one on the scene. It's proper seamanship to be prepared to tow another vessel in distress. On the other hand, even though as a proper seaman, you maintain your boat well and generally know how to avoid trouble, things do occasionally go wrong nonetheless, and the possibility remains that you may need a tow someday. It's a dogfish-eat-dogfish world out there, so be prepared to tow and be towed.

TOWING ASTERN

Most professional towboats sport a centered, aft towing post that is integral to the structure of the boat. This post allows the boat to take the sometimes incredible strain of a tow without having hardware pull loose. Its central location allows it to be used whether the boat is towing off its port or starboard side, so a single hefty towing hauser can remain belayed to it all the time. And its location near the boat's pivot point ensures that the boat retains optimum steering control when pulling a load. All in all, it's a great thing for a towboat.

Odds are, however, that your boat doesn't have a centered-aft towing post, and you'll be reduced to using your stern cleats. It is far better to use both cleats at once, to halve the strain on them. In order to do this, you need to rig a bridle. In fact, you should rig bridles at *both* ends of the towline.

A towing post on a RIB-type towboat.

The bridle on the towboat should be nylon—either three-strand or braided dockline is ideal. Use the largest diameter line that will allow you to make a complete turn around the base of an aft cleat and a figure eight and half hitch around the cleat's horns. But don't cleat it off yet. Start with the other end, which should have a loop in it. A made-up dockline with a spliced eye is perfect; otherwise, tie a bowline at one end. Put this end of the bridle over the other stern cleat. Doing it this way serves two purposes:

- One end of the bridle remains fixed, so all adjustments in the bridle's length are made at the other end. Tie it off with sufficient slack to clear aft obstructions such as flagstaffs and outboard engines.

- The fixed end leaves enough room on the cleat to tie off the bitter end of the towline with a figure eight on the same cleat. This allows the length of the towline to be adjusted from the towboat as discussed below.

To further distribute the strain on the bridle, or if you're unsure about the backing of the stern cleats, an additional line can be looped around the base of the stern cleats and then led forward to the midships and/or forward cleats. If there were to be a failure of the stern cleats, the other cleats would take up the strain. I don't recommend setting up the bridle directly from the midships cleats however, as I've found that it adversely affects the maneuverability of the towboat.

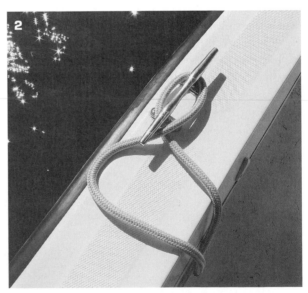

Rigging a towline. 1. The towline is belayed utilizing figure-eight turns and half hitches to cleats forward of the stern cleats in order to spread the strain. 2. A complete turn, a figure eight, and two half hitches on a horn cleat will ensure that nylon or Dacron line—which can become "slippery" and slide free under strain—stays wrapped around the cleat. Here's the first wrap around the base of the cleat.

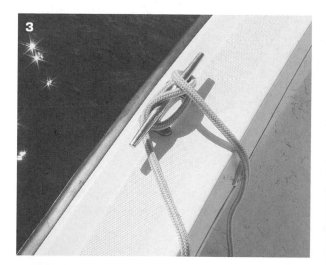

3. The first wrap is completed and the line is brought around the horn of the cleat to form a figure-eight wrap. 4. A turn of the line is brought under the wrap to form the first half hitch. 5. The end of the line is brought under the wrap on the other horn to form the second half hitch.

Use a similar size dockline for the towed boat's bridle. An eye or bowline at one end is nice to have but not essential, since, unlike on the towboat, the length of the bridle on the towed vessel does not need be adjusted once it's in place. All adjustments are made at the towboat.

If the towed boat has two bow cleats, lead the bridle line through the bow chocks and secure both ends to the cleats, leaving enough slack to clear any bow appurtenances, such as pulpits and anchor supports. As the strength of the bow cleats on towed vessels are unknown factors, it is best to spread the strain to the boat's midships cleats and/or aft cleats. Take two additional lines and secure them to the bridle, just forward of each cleat, with rolling hitches (see Chapter 6). Lead these lines to the midships and/or aft cleat on the same side, placing some tension on the line and tying them off with figure eights.

If the towed boat has a single, centrally placed bow cleat and bow chocks, secure the bridle line through the bow chocks and secure both ends to the cleat, leaving the bridle long enough to clear any obstructions. The towline will be secured to the bridle forward of the stem, which will minimize chafe to the towline from the bow chocks.

If the towed boat has no bow chocks, the towline can be secured directly to the bow cleat via a loop or utilizing a full turn around the base of the cleat, followed by a figure eight and a half hitch. In this situation, the towline must be chafe-protected wherever it comes in contact with any part of either boat and closely monitored for chafe during the tow. While the ideal chafe protection is a length of rubber garden hose split lengthwise and placed over the line (it can be held in place by strips of duct tape at the ends), anything that will protect the line from chafe will help. Rags held in place by duct tape will do, or even duct tape by itself—although duct tape will wear quickly and have to be replaced regularly.

Because of the great strain applied to a single bow cleat, additional lines should be established to spread the strain to the midships and/or stern cleats.

Preparing the Towline

The towline should be the same material (nylon) and diameter as the bridles. Anchor lines make good towlines, once chain leads and anchors are detached.

The towline should be at least 150 feet long. This will provide sufficient length for tying off at both ends, with 100 feet of towing line in use and 30 to 50 feet available for adjustment. Professional towers often use a large snap hook secured to the end of the towline that will be passed to the disabled boat. You may use a snap hook or a shackle if either is available, but neither is essential.

Secure the towline by placing three or four rolling turns of the towline around the center of the bridle and then belay it with a figure eight to the aft cleat with the looped end of the bridle around it. The primary strain will remain at the center of the bridle, while that aft cleat will just serve to tie off the excess line.

Coil the towline so that the end to be passed to the towed boat is on top. Also coil the excess line that will remain on the towing boat for adjustment.

Passing the Towline

Ideally, the towboat should approach the disabled vessel from leeward (downwind). This allows the towboat more control if it has to maneuver quickly to avoid a collision. If the towboat approaches from windward—the wind setting it down upon the incapacitated vessel—there is a greater possibility of damage or injury due to miscalculation.

Again, ideally, the crew of the towing boat should be able to hand the towline—rather than toss it—to the crew of the other vessel. To gain a few extra feet of reach, the line can be secured to the end of a boathook and passed over that way.

If high winds or rough seas make it impractical to hand over the towline, then the towboat must approach from windward and the line should be tossed to the disabled

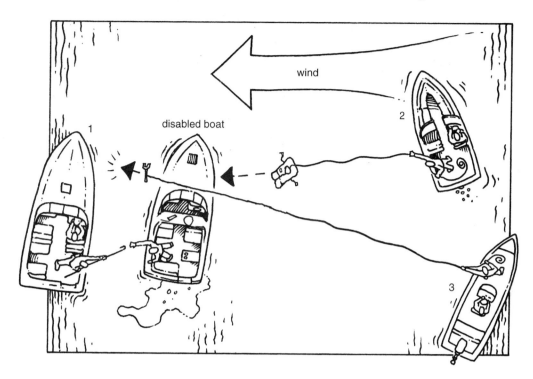

Three methods of getting a towline to another vessel. 1. Approach from downwind and pass the towline to a deckhand by hand or with a boathook. 2. Approach from upwind. Tie the line to a fender or a PFD, and let it drift down to the disabled boat. 3. Approach from upwind. Tie the line to a heavy object and throw it over (not at) the disabled vessel.

vessel. The operator of the towboat must be especially cautious, as the wind and sea are acting to set his boat toward the other vessel and more room will be needed to maneuver clear.

If it is impractical to approach the disabled vessel close enough to heave the towline, secure a line of smaller diameter—a *heaving* line—to the end of the larger towline and tie a weight, possibly a wrench or hammer, to the other end. While there are a number of preferred knots that are designed to bend two lines of different diameters together, the simplest way to attach the heaving line to the towline is to bend them together using bowlines at the ends of each. After the crew of the disabled vessel is warned to stay clear, toss the heaving line to the other boat. It's a good idea, especially if using a weight such as a hammer or heavy wrench, to toss the heaving line *over* the boat instead of directly at it. The disabled boat's crew can then use the heaving line to haul in the towline.

Another way to get the towline to the disabled vessel is for the towing vessel to lie upwind from the disabled boat and float the towline down on a fender or personal flotation device. Care must be taken that the line does not get engaged in the towboat's prop. For that same reason, it is not advisable to drag the towline to the disabled vessel without proper flotation of the towline. The most common mishap during these types of maneuvers is the Good Samaritan's vessel becomes disabled due to a line in its prop.

Once the end of the towline is aboard the disabled vessel, its crew should attach it to the bridle with the snaphook or shackle, if it is so equipped. If not, then a bowline should be used, but it may be worthwhile to establish first that the crew does, in fact, know how to tie a bowline. This is not a good place to tie a rolling hitch. The shackle or bowline allows the tow rope to slide on the disabled boat's bridle, thus centering the pull on both ends of the bridle regardless of the relative angles of the two boats. The result is a more efficient tow and less strain on a single cleat.

Taking the Strain

Once the towline is securely established between the two bridles, station a crewmember aft to manage the line. While the towboat gets slowly under way, the crewmember aft pays out line by allowing the rolling turns previously placed around the bridle to feed smoothly, preventing excess slack from entering the water and preventing the line from becoming kinked, tangled, or—worse—wrapped around the towboat's propeller. (You *certainly* don't want two disabled boats attached to each other, particularly if there's a sea running.) The deployment of the line will be under more control if it is fed around one or both horns of the aft cleat. Keep paying out line until the boats are separated by two or three boat lengths.

The line is secured when the crewmember on the towboat determines that the two boats are "in sequence"—both boats are on the crests of two waves at the same time. A moment later, both boats will be in troughs at the same time. This is important. If the boats are out of sequence, the line will jerk and possibly snap due to the stresses of two boats pitching and yawing out of synch. While I suggested two or three boat lengths, the most practical length will be determined by trial and error and the sea state during the tow. It is important, however, to maintain the "in sequence" nature of the tow; the longer the towline, especially in rougher seas, the more difficult it will be to keep both boats in the troughs or on crests at the same time.

It is the responsibility of the skipper of the towed boat to steer for the center of the transom of the towing boat. The more the towed boat slews off center, the more it will pull the towing boat off course. In high seas, this could invite a broach. For the purpose of

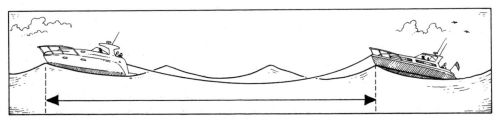

Towing with both boats "in sequence" on swells.

minimizing strain and safety, the towing boat should always be operated at the slowest practical speed. In addition, when maneuvering, the skipper of the towboat should communicate his intentions to the skipper of the towed boat so that he can adjust the rudder to assist with the turn. Otherwise, the towed boat can be "jerked" around and difficult to control.

The towboat should be maneuvered in keeping with its capabilities and limitations. For instance, when towing with a single-screw vessel with a right-hand prop, remember that the boat normally turns easier to starboard than to port while coming ahead. A turn to port will be even more unwieldy when towing. When towing with twins, the engines can be used during maneuvering, such as increasing power to the starboard engine when turning to port. Regardless of the type of boat, it goes without saying that you'll have to go much slower than usual and exhibit extreme care in all maneuvers.

Under the Rules of the Road, certain lights and day shapes are required to be shown when towing. These can be looked up in the appropriate publications, such as *Chapman's Seamanship* or *One-Minute Guide to the Rules of the Road* by Charlie Wing (see page 89). Most recreational boats, however, are not equipped to show these signals, and, in my opinion, the fact that a recreational vessel has another boat under tow indicates a certain level of emergency or necessity. So I can't imagine the Coast Guard coming down on you for a failure to display the proper lights or shapes. Nonetheless, given the nature of the situation, I would regularly transmit a Sécurité call (see Chapter 3).

Crews on both boats must not stand in line with the towline. In the event of the line snapping or a cleat tearing loose, there can be a dangerous "slingshot effect."

To lengthen the towline while under way, partially uncleat it at the towboat end and allow it to ease out. To shorten the line, the towing boat must lose way so there's no strain at all on the towline. It can then be taken in and resecured.

Casting Off and Towing "on the Hip"

You've made it into harbor. Good job! To separate the boats, the towboat comes to a complete stop and the engines are taken out of gear. The crew of the towed boat is then directed to cast off the line, and the crew of the towboat quickly retrieves and coils it on deck before reengaging its engines.

At this point, a commercial tower will usually secure the disabled boat alongside and ease it up to the dock or final destination. Towing alongside like this, or "on the hip," gives the towboat the best maneuverability. (See the following section for details.) But docking a towed boat can be a tricky maneuver for the nonprofessional and is best avoided, if possible. Ideally, the towed boat—under a shortened towline—can be cast off close enough to the dock for a line to be sent ashore and the boat brought in manually. Alternatively, the towed boat can drop an anchor in a safe location and wait until a yard boat can tow it in. Be aware, however, that if the boat's engine is out, setting the hook may be problematic.

If it is necessary for the towboat to come alongside to bring the disabled boat closer to its berth, take care that appurtenances such as flybridges, tuna towers, pulpits, and so on, are not in danger of contact. Both boats should be fendered, and spring lines rigged from the bow cleat of the towing boat to the midships cleat of the towed boat as well as from the stern cleat of the towed boat to the midships cleat on the towing boat. Breast lines are also arranged between both boats' bow cleats and both boats' stern cleats. The towboat should then maneuver the towed boat close enough to the dock so that a line or crew can be set ashore. The towboat should not attempt to place the disabled boat against the dock. If conditions are anything other than calm, it is best to seek professional help. As a general rule, when any distance is to be covered, it's best to tow astern, as no matter how securely boats are secured alongside each other, wave or wake action can cause damage.

TOWING WITH A DINGHY

A 1960s-era Chris Craft Constellation has the unique lines and profile of a classic yacht—the kind of shape that makes you stop what you're doing and look up when it makes its stately procession down the waterway. The familiar, fully restored Connie that I was admiring as it appeared through an early morning fog on Connecticut's Mystic River was moving with its accustomed grace, but the sound effects were all wrong. Instead of the measured throb of the twin Cummins diesels that I knew it had been re-powered with, there was the high-pitched clatter of a single, hardworking 35-horsepower Johnson outboard.

Then I noticed that the Johnson was attached to a thoroughly contemporary 13-foot Boston Whaler, which I recognized as the Chris's tender, which was itself lashed to the Connie's stern quarter. It turned out that the Constellation had lost power while out on Long Island Sound (a victim of bad fuel, which could be a discussion in itself), and the skipper had hauled it all the way back with the tender. For the long haul back, he had towed astern—utilizing a bridled towline from the aft cleats of the Whaler to the Connie's bow cleat. But when he came into the narrow confines of the Mystic River, he had lashed the tender alongside for the added maneuverability in close quarters that "towing on the hip" allows.

Towing a larger boat astern or alongside with an outboard powered tender is a common practice with many working boatyards. It is a quick and handy way to get the beast from one point to the other without utilizing the mains. While it's not something that we, as recreational boaters, would prefer to do, there can be times—as my friend with the Connie discovered—when the need arises. As with any tow, the preferred method is "line astern" if there is any distance to be covered and especially when the waters are anything other than calm. A tender lashed alongside a disabled vessel—as discussed below—is particularly susceptible to seas and wave action.

When towing line astern with the dinghy, the towlines should be set up, bridled, and secured as already discussed—in the same way as when towing with a larger boat. For the control needed for close-in maneuvering, the tender should be lashed alongside the larger vessel—a maneuver that shouldn't be attempted unless the water is relatively calm.

The dink—be it inboard- or outboard-powered, solid hull, inflatable, or RIB—should be lashed on the aft quarter of the mother ship, with the prop(s) a foot or two aft of the

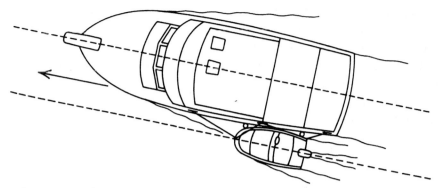

When you need to tow a large vessel with a dinghy, don't do it on the end of a towline. Lashing the two boats together with bow, stern, and spring lines will give much better control. (Bruce Alderson)

stern of the towed vessel. This places the pivot point of the two joined vessels farther aft, allowing for more efficient maneuvering. The dink can be tied on either side, keeping in mind that the tow will turn more efficiently to the side opposite where the dink is lashed. Therefore, if a hard turn to starboard is anticipated, the dink will be most efficient if it's lashed on the port quarter. If the disabled boat is considerably larger than the dink, or if the tender's outboard is underpowered for the job (only trial and error will tell), a turn in the direction of the side the dink is lashed may be impossible, especially if wind or current are in opposition. With good teamwork between a person on board the larger vessel and the operator of the dinghy, the dinghy can zip around and be re-lashed quickly from one side to the other. During any turning maneuver, an offset of the rudder of the towed boat will be of assistance.

Tying up the dinghy to the disabled vessel is the same as if you were securing the tender to a dock. Spring lines are particularly important as they will be doing most of the work. Fore-and-aft springs should be tied to strong points on the dink—mooring cleats—as well as to securely backed cleats on the towed boat. Bow, stern, and breast lines should be tied as tightly as possible to prevent any extraneous movement. Of course, if it's a hard dink, fenders need to be placed between the boats.

If you're towing with an inflatable, pay close attention to where you're attaching the lines. Many inflatables have no cleats or proper line attachments. I've tied lines to wooden seats and their brackets and then looped the line around all the seats so the strain is evenly distributed. If necessary, a mooring line can circle the entire dink, with attachments at its bow towing ring and its outboard bracket. With any inflatable, it's important that it be inflated to the maximum recommended pressure. In fact, it should be inflated to the max at all times.

Like everything else in our field, it's always best to practice the maneuvers discussed here before you need to do them so that when the oil does hit the fan and fast action is a must, you're prepared.

8
Staying Cool in Emergencies

THE POSSIBILITY OF A DISASTER while under way brings out the deepest fears of those who love boating. Thinking ahead and being prepared are the best ways to calm those fears. Responding rationally is what this chapter and the next are about—they take the admittedly disturbing subject of emergencies (mechanical failures, fire at sea, carbon monoxide poisoning, and so on) and categorize them so that each can be dealt with logically and effectively in the clinch.

How do we prepare for emergencies when our main objective as pleasure boaters is to, well, experience pleasure on the water? Of course, preparation itself is key. This includes having the boat in great condition at the beginning of every boating season and making sure that all is well before leaving the dock, *every time*. It also includes knowing what steps to take when things go wrong, so you can prevent emergencies from deteriorating into catastrophes. But the simplest and most effective preventative measure—whether fishing, cruising, pulling a skier, or just plain having fun aboard—is to be aware of our boat, aware of our surroundings, and aware of ourselves, our passengers, and our crew.

Simple steps like eyeballing the engines both before and after they fire up can expose a whole array of potential problems. While the hatch is up, check out the prop/transmission shaft marriage. Bolts should be snugged down and properly safety-wired. Once the engines have started up, look, listen, and smell. Here's where you'll spot flapping belts; the warning mist of spraying fuel, water, and oil; or the unmistakable odor of hot antifreeze that indicates a cooling system leak.

The time to be aware of problems is at the dock, before you get under way. Put the engine into gear while still tied up. Listen for any "clunk" that may indicate a transmission on its way out. Watch the shafts spinning, looking for improperly secured wires and hosing dangerously close to the shafts, as well as excessive leakage from the shaft glands—or not enough. With dripless glands it's a good idea to place your hands over the spinning shafts, if you can reach them, to feel if they are putting out heat. If they are, it's an indication that the shafts aren't being properly lubricated. (If you have a twin-engine installation with dripless water-lubricated glands, you can have a "cross-over hose" installed. This will provide cooling water from one gland to the other, so that, if you're running on one engine, the other shaft will continue to receive lubrication and you won't have to restrict it from turning.)

There are more preventative and safety measures that we can take—and we'll discuss them as we go along. But, like venting the bilges before firing up, observing the engines while they're running is a good beginning for everything that follows.

TOOLS AND SUPPLIES TO HAVE ABOARD

The amount of tools to be kept aboard is only limited by the intended purpose of the vessel and the crew's mechanical abilities. A long-legged cruiser operated by a trained mechanic is going to carry tools and supplies of greater complexity than one run by a casual boater on trips in protected waters. Every boat, however, should carry replacement hoses, belts, and impellers as well as the tools to install them. With the wide availability of multipurpose marine-grade tool kits, it is poor seamanship not to have such a kit aboard. The following tools and supplies comprise a basic and compact tool kit that can help you out of many emergencies:

- Socket sets, metric and standard (For periodic tightening of hose clamps, $\frac{3}{16}$-inch and $\frac{3}{8}$-inch sockets are invaluable.)
- Complete set of open and closed-end metric and standard-sized wrenches
- Allen wrench sets, metric and standard
- Pocket knife with standard and serrated blades (I like Leatherman-style multi-tools for the variety of "blades," and lock-back knives for their simplicity and safety.)
- Slotted and Phillips-head screwdrivers, various sizes
- Locking pliers (e.g., Vise-Grips)
- Extended jaw (water pump) pliers
- Hammers, claw-type and ball-peen
- Metal and wood files
- Hacksaw with wood, plastic, and metal blades
- Bolt cutter
- Electrical kit, including wire cutters and various wire connectors
- Electrical and duct tape

- Tapered wood plugs
- Bedding compound
- Structural adhesive
- Measuring tape
- All-stainless hose clamps in sizes for all fuel and water hosing aboard

FIRST STEPS IN AN EMERGENCY

In every incident that might result in the loss of the boat, whether through water incursion, fire, or otherwise, the first step is to ensure the crew's safety. Regardless of the nature or intensity of the emergency, there are no exceptions. It is the captain's responsibility to see that all aboard are issued personal flotation devices (PFDs) and made to put them on; are aware of the location of throwable and floatable devices; and are versed in the deployment of the life raft. (See Chapter 10.)

The next step is to write down the vessel's location. In every emergency, there is a possibility of electronics failures. If you can read the latitude/longitude on the GPS as soon as the incident occurs, do so immediately and write it down, so that you can communicate it to the Coast Guard or other boats if and when necessary. (It is good seamanship and common sense to be able to obtain your position instantly at any moment during any passage.)

At this point, the captain may consider delegating responsibilities, depending on the number and capabilities of those aboard. Listed here are some of the tasks that may need to be addressed. There are a lot of them—possibly too many to do yourself efficaciously—so get help from your passengers or crew. You can't fight a fire or plug a leak at the same time that you're helping a child into his PFD or treating a concussion.

- Distribute PFDs and ensure that they're put on properly
- Man the helm
- Maintain radio watch; transmit distress call
- Maintain lookout
- Administer first aid
- Assist children, the elderly, and incapacitated personnel with PFDs and whatever necessary for their particular needs
- Prepare life raft for deployment
- Repair damage
- Fight fire

As soon as feasible, a VHF radio call should be initiated, alerting the Coast Guard or nearby vessels that there is a problem aboard. Two types of calls are recognized, depending upon the nature of the emergency:

1. If the boat is not in *immediate and grave danger,* the Marine Urgency call can be transmitted. This call, commonly known as the Pan-Pan (the *a* is pronounced "ah"), is used if the emergency is not life- or vessel-threatening, and there is a possibility of making port or of the crew being able to make repairs. With this call, you are alerting authorities and other vessels that there is a situation occurring that might deteriorate and might require assistance. The call consists of the term *Pan-Pan* repeated three times as follows: "Pan-Pan, Pan-Pan, Pan-Pan; this is the vessel _____ at (latitude/longitude) calling the United States Coast Guard." When the Coast Guard answers, immediately transmit your position and the nature of the emergency. If you cannot contact the Coast Guard, transmit the Pan-Pan again to "any vessel" and request the answering vessel to contact the Coast Guard or, if it is unable to do so, to remain in contact with you.

2. If the boat is in immediate and grave danger (for example, if there is a possibility of the vessel foundering) and assistance is needed immediately, transmit the Mayday call. The script is basically the same as above, with *Mayday* replacing *Pan-Pan.* If you receive no response, wait 30 seconds and repeat the call. Transmit the vessel's name, the nature of the emergency, and the latitude/longitude each time the Mayday is transmitted.

THINGS THAT BREAK

As so often happens at sea, the failure of one component creates a problem, but then things that are seemingly unrelated begin to go awry. It's only upon retrospect that the clues and the missed warnings add up—as the delivery crew of a 50-foot motoryacht discovered to their chagrin.

The boat was fresh from the factory, and the delivery was to be from Melbourne, Florida, to Annapolis, Maryland. The skipper, an old delivery hand, had performed a diligent examination of the boat—a good idea as the trip would include long offshore jumps. In the course of his exam, he noted that the platform the boat's genset was mounted on didn't look too sturdily constructed. It was built of $\frac{7}{8}$-inch plywood glassed over and tabbed to a bulkhead and perceptibly vibrated when the mains and the generator were running. He didn't take any action as he assumed that the builder, an experienced and reputable yard, knew what it was doing and had installed it properly, in spite of its appearance. Later, when the delivery captain discussed the trip with the factory rep, the rep suggested that if the matter had been brought to the builder's attention, it would have been determined that the platform had been installed improperly and the situation corrected.

But that was to be learned in the future. In the here and now, while running a few miles off North Carolina's Beaufort Inlet, the boat slammed into one sea too many. A crash was heard from below followed by the sound of high voltage sparking, the acrid odor of burnt wires, and the sight of billowing smoke from the engine room, which was followed by a total electric failure. The automatic fire suppression system functioned as designed and extinguished the blaze quickly, but for three hours in the pre-dawn of a cold November day, the boat rolled sickeningly in the swell until the crew was able to safely vent and enter the engine room.

Of course, the platform had collapsed, following the failure of the poorly applied tabbing; and the genset, in falling, had shorted against one engine, destroying its starter and alternator and frying most of the wiring and circuit breakers. Fortunately, one isolated household battery had survived the carnage, and eventually the crew was able to get an engine started and make port.

Among the lessons learned was that there is no such thing as a minor problem at sea. If a malfunction, or a potential problem, is noted, it must be addressed. And the importance of observation cannot be overstated. On naval and commercial vessels, hourly engine checks are part of the watch routine—not a bad idea for any boat under way. The postmortem of the motoryacht showed that anything more than a cursory glance while under way would have shown crazing in the tabbing that eventually led to failure and increasing vibration of the genset platform. The properly alarmed crew then would have avoided an expensive, embarrassing, and potentially dangerous delay.

Structural Failures

By definition, every structural component of a powerboat is subjected to stress of one sort or another. (By "structural," I'm referring to pieces that are built permanently into the hull—items including hull-deck joints, engine beds, genset supports, and bulkheads.) Although most powerboats are well-built and reliable, it is inevitable that structural problems will arise now and then. Light weight is prized by owners, so designers are always under pressure to cut weight to the maximum extent possible, and, occasionally, they overdo it. Most boats are built in fairly small quantities, and many are subject to a high degree of customization, both during construction and years later, so the odds of a structural engineering error showing up on *your* boat are fairly high, compared to, say, an automobile. Because virtually all powerboats are built by hand, there's always the possibility of a worker making a mistake due to carelessness or ignorance. And its very use subjects the boat's structures to vibration, slamming loads, sheer, torque, and numerous other forces.

No wonder things break on occasion! Engine beds, genset shelving, bulkheads, and hull-deck joints should all be monitored when under way for cracks, broken tabbing, and gelcoat crazing—all signs of failure or degradation. And they should all be examined at least annually, or when the boat is undergoing maintenance.

Usually, hull and deck or laminate separations occur during hard running and are the result of improper design or shoddy building practices. Less often, because previous repairs or poorly bedded deck hardware have allowed water to intrude into the core of the deck laminate, the core has rotted to mush, and so the deck itself has lost its structural integrity. A thorough and responsible pre-purchase survey—including a history of the boat's previous service—should uncover both flaws and causative factors. Warning signs include "oil-canning" or flexing of the hull upon being blocked; buckling and "give" in decks when being walked upon; and crazing and bubbling of the hull.

This structural damage was caused by poor layup of the laminate during manufacturing. Special dye was used to make the stress cracks show up clearly. (BoatU.S.)

Inspection while under way is also critically important. The movement of an engine due to failure of the bed supports can create strain on the transmission/shaft coupling and the stuffing box, which can fail and lead to a serious leak. A hull-deck joint that begins to separate while under way allows a serious incursion of water and substantially reduces the overall strength of the hull, which could easily lead to a cascade of structural problems. We've already seen the kinds of near-disaster than can arise from a broken genset shelf. Here's what to look for:

- Engine beds: "dancing" of engine upon beds; working or vibration of bed supports
- Genset supports: crazed gelcoating; cracks in tabbing; play in support legs
- Hull-deck joints: broken or missing fasteners; unseated molding over the joint; leaks
- Bulkhead-to-hull joints: cracking or crazing of gelcoat or overlying paint; unusual noises (groaning, cracking, squeaking) while under way

If engine mounts are loose or detached, the affected engine must be shut down immediately. It may be feasible to wedge and block the engine in place, but it is imperative to

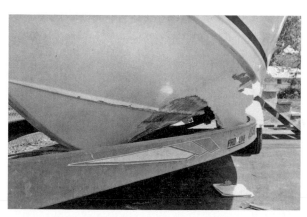

Farther aft on the same boat, the laminate has actually begun breaking apart—the result of poor layup plus probably very hard usage. (BoatU.S.)

maintain the alignment of the shaft, and it is virtually impossible to do this without starting up the engine and putting it in gear. If, upon doing so, you notice unusual vibration or excessive weeping of the stern gland, shut down the engine immediately and attempt to correct the situation—although, without specialized tools, it may be impossible to determine the direction of the misalignment. If the boat has a single engine and shutting it down will place it or the crew in danger, reduce speed to the minimum to maintain way and shut down as soon as feasible.

If a shelf supporting a genset, pump, or other piece of equipment is coming loose, reduce speed immediately. Turn off the machinery that the shelving supports, and place items beneath it to provide additional support. You can use such items as tool kit boxes, life jackets, spare bedding, and seat cushions. Shelving supports can be emergency-braced by duct taping boathooks or mop handles that have been cut down to make "splints" alongside.

You simply can't do much about a failing hull-deck or bulkhead-to-hull joint except to reduce speed and return to port. Broken or separated tabbing requires fiberglass repair that is generally impractical while under way, and hull-deck fasteners are frequently inaccessible. After you get in, take immediate steps to have the problem repaired and don't use the boat until you've done so. The failure of these structural items could impose additional strain on other parts of the boat, leading to further failures.

Bolt-On Failures

Bolted-on accessories, such as tuna towers, some flybridge structures, windshield bases and supports, stanchions, and seats, can be extremely hazardous if they come adrift. Once a seat base or a stanchion gets loose, it will rapidly become looser with continued use, and this will cause, at the minimum, avoidable damage to the deck and/or hardware and, at the other extreme, catastrophic failure at the least opportune time—such as when you're leaning hard against it to keep your balance. Likewise, a tuna tower that comes loose can do spectacular damage to everything and everyone around it; a loose dinghy davit could drop the boat and its passengers; and a poorly secured windshield could come adrift and fly back at the helmsperson while the boat is under way at speed.

As noted, many such failures are the result of improper installation with poorly applied bedding. Another frequent cause is the failure to maintain the boat properly—to examine it carefully, find loose fittings, and tighten them before things get worse. Look for movement or "working" of the supports, loose nuts and bolts, and movement or "dancing" of screw heads in supports while under way.

A loose component under stress will "work" until it loses its bedding compound—at which time it will allow water into the core and things will quickly go downhill from there. But find something as soon as any signs of looseness appear, and you'll probably be able to quickly rescue the situation. You really should be able to throw your whole weight against a stanchion or seat with no movement or unusual squeaking or creaking. Even so, some "looseness" might not be evident, so look also for indicators such as gelcoat crazing

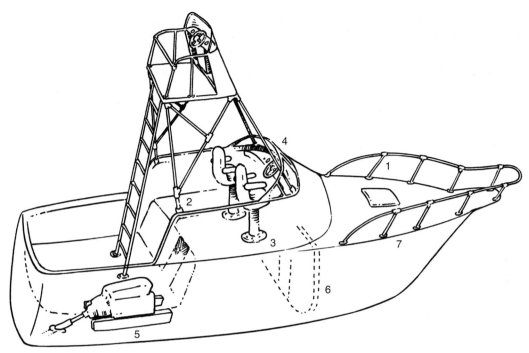

Things that break include bolt-ons such as: 1. stanchions, 2. tuna towers, 3. seat bases, 4. windshields, and structural items like 5. engine beds and genset shelving, 6. bulkhead-hull joints, and 7. hull-deck joints.

around the base of the bolted-on component or hardened globs of dried-out bedding compound that has squeezed from beneath the base onto the deck.

If, in spite of your vigilance, something begins to come adrift, reduce speed immediately and see if you can tighten it up. It may be simply a matter of torquing down on the nuts—an argument for having complete sets of wrenches and sockets on board at all times. Often, however, the nuts won't tighten down because the threads may have been damaged. Or, if poor quality hardware was used, it may be corroded in situ. In that case, do whatever you must to remove and extract the old fasteners—use a cold chisel, hacksaw, hammer and drift, or whatever—and replace them with good stainless fasteners.

It may be that you can tighten up the existing hardware holding down a stanchion or seat base, but that still doesn't immobilize the component itself. Possibly, the bolt holes have widened due to prolonged "working." You might be able to make things solid again by using larger-diameter fasteners through the larger holes.

If one end of a nut-bolt fastening is inaccessible and the fastening can't be removed or replaced, use any available means to support or restrict the structure—rope, wood bracing, and duct tape are a few options. Don't have any spare two-by-fours aboard for bracing? In a true emergency, you'll likely find plenty of wood aboard in seat bases, cabinetry, furniture, and so on. Have at it with hammers, axes, or whatever it takes to make the repair!

A Jury-Rig Saves the Day

UNUSUAL CIRCUMSTANCES often demand unusual remedies, and mariners frequently have to resort to unorthodox procedures when near-disaster strikes. Indeed, "to jury-rig"—the nautical version of making do with whatever is available—has become part of the lexicon. The delivery crew of a new 32-foot sportfisherman took advantage of an age-old procedure to address an unexpected structural problem.

Rounding Cape Hatteras in moderate head seas on a voyage from North Carolina to New Jersey, the crew heard unusual creaking and groaning sounds from the flybridge supports and noticed first a crazing followed by a cracking of the fiberglass at the flybridge/deck joint. Fastenings of the attached tuna

tower began to pull from the deck. In a short time it became obvious that the boat's motion could cause a complete rupture of the structure.

Thinking quickly, the skipper gathered all the dock and anchor lines together and tied parallel lines from various points on the tuna tower to well-backed points on the deck, such as the windlass and bow, midships, and stern cleats. Then utilizing long-handled wrenches, taped-together sections of mops and boathooks, and the handle of the electric/manual windlass, he created a number of Spanish windlasses to exert tension on the lines to support the tower/flybridge structure. It worked well enough for the boat to proceed to its intended port.

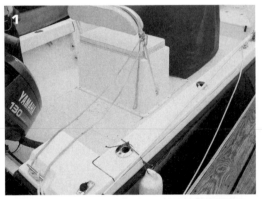

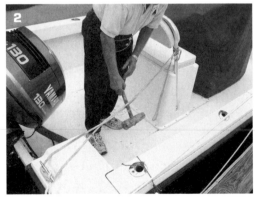

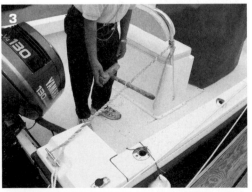

Rigging a Spanish windlass. 1. The line is being set up for a Spanish windlass. 2. A twist is applied with a shaft (here a mallet handle) passed between the runs of line. 3. The structure is supported in place by the tension applied with the Spanish windlass.

If a tuna tower or bolted-on flybridge becomes adrift while under way, reduce speed immediately. Get the crew down, remove as much topside weight as possible, and operate the boat from a lower station as you return to port. If there is a possibility of safe haven running downwind/-sea, that should be the preferred route, as the more severe motion of running into seas will exacerbate the problem. In the interim, see if you can make repairs, or at least restrict the tower's movement. If through-bolted fittings are reachable, determine if backing nuts or plates have worked loose and, if so, attempt to replace or re-bolt.

There have been instances of poorly secured windshields breaking loose, flying back, and causing serious injury. As always, if you detect a problem while under way, reduce speed. If the windshield has a "walk-through" section to the foredeck, close and latch that section; it will create added support.

Special attention should be paid to davit arms when running in seas. Because of the high leverage from the cantilevered load that they support, they must be tightly secured to prevent movement. Backing plates should be regularly inspected. When under way, especially in seas, swing davit arms inboard and lash them in place to prevent movement. During inspection, look for crazing of the deck around the bases.

The nuts that secure the bolts on most pedestal-type seats and stanchions are frequently hidden behind headliners and/or trim and it is impractical to attempt a repair while under way. If you can't tighten or replace the nuts and bolts, try to avoid using them. Stand rather than sit on a wobbly seat that might collapse under you, and if you must go forward, use the side deck that *doesn't* have the bad stanchion.

Stress damage to a stanchion base.

Wiring and Hosing

Wiring that is properly "loomed" is supported by tie wraps or is bracketed to bulkheads at intervals along its run without sagging or taking sharp turns. Wiring should be chafe-protected by rubber grommets or similar material wherever it passes through bulkheads or comes in contact with hard surfaces or areas prone to vibration. Look for separation of pin or butt connectors and chafing of the covering over wires. While under way, observe wiring for movement, slack, or looseness near moving machinery.

All hosing ends should be double-clamped with 100 percent stainless steel hose clamps. (Many stainless steel hose clamps have plain steel screws that are subject to corrosion. Make sure you get clamps that are *all* stainless steel, found at marine suppliers.) Periodically check the tightness of clamps with a screwdriver or nut driver (most hose clamp nuts are $5/16$-inch or $3/8$-inch). Hosing, also, should be chafe protected wherever it comes into contact with or passes through bulkheads or other hard surfaces. Any hosing that curves or takes a sharp turn should be considered suspect for failure. Observe the surface of hosing; if it looks "ragged" or shows cracking between the ridges, it should be replaced as soon as possible.

Any repair that necessitates the removal of wiring or hosing that can incapacitate the boat (removing engine cooling hosing from its seacock or through-hull fitting, for instance) should not be attempted unless the boat cannot return to port safely without the repair. Do not attempt any electrical or plumbing repairs while nearby machinery is operating. If time allows, utilize proper ends and connectors for electrical repairs rather than relying solely on electrical tape. Before removing or working on hosing, close the necessary seacocks and determine that the contents aren't under pressure.

Wires should be properly routed and secured every 18 inches. These weren't. They chafed, shorted out, and caused a fire. (BoatU.S.)

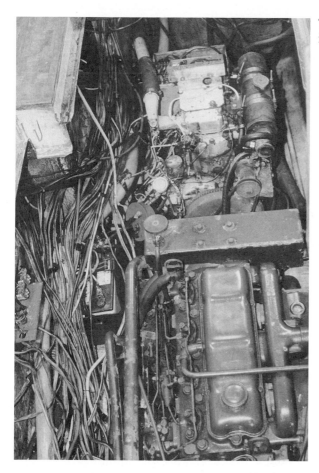

This spaghetti-style wiring is a fire waiting to happen. (BoatU.S.)

FIRE AT SEA

The 102-foot motoryacht had finally left port after an extensive renovation in a Florida yard and began its long offshore trek to Newport, Rhode Island. As is common after a layup, there was still plenty of refinishing and detail work to be performed while under way. The experienced crew quickly fell into an efficient shipboard routine—cleaning, painting, varnishing, and polishing—working through the morning before breaking for lunch.

At that point, the skipper walked through the saloon. He stopped momentarily dead in his tracks and then immediately recalled the crew and assembled them in the saloon surrounding its centerpiece: a gorgeous table intricately inlaid with exotic woods. He focused their attention on a large charred spot in the table's center. A rag saturated with furniture polish had been left there, and in the midst of a group of five dedicated and conscientious workers, a vagrant sunbeam had found its way in, focused on the rag, and did the spontaneous combustion thing. The skipper pointed out in no uncertain terms what the result could have been had the sunbeam been left to do its work uninterrupted.

The moral of this story, of course, goes beyond not leaving oil-saturated rags on your dining room table. Basically, it's that you cannot be vigilant enough when it comes to fire prevention. According to Coast Guard and boating industry literature, the percentage of boat fires caused by spontaneous combustion is statistically negligible (although at about the same time, a raging conflagration in a New Jersey boatyard resulted from that very cause). However, if that fire had gotten out of hand, those statistics would have been meaningless to the owner of that yacht.

So what *is* the number one cause of boat fires? Shorts in the DC wiring. According to Coast Guard statistics, 90 percent of those shorts, and subsequent fires, occur in the engine compartment—and you don't have to be a world-class surveyor to figure out why. The wires are bundled together in a hot environment; they get old and brittle; and often they're painted over, making it harder to spot breaks and bare spots. Especially on older boats, wires are installed in relatively inaccessible areas and often become coated in flammable grease. And all this occurs in a vibrating environment that promotes chafe. Fuses and breakers? Sure, they're a great line of defense, but often the damage is well under way by the time they do their thing. The trick, of course, is periodic and ongoing inspection and maintenance.

AC electrics account for the next most frequent cause of fires. You can attribute these fires to the same causes as the DC wires, adding AC's higher voltage. The top AC fire causer? The answer is the electric heater—especially when it is served by chafed wires; does not automatically shut off when tipped over; or is surrounded by flammables such as bedding, upholstery, or dry wood trim. Also of concern are shore power connections, both on the dock and aboard. Exposed to the elements and stressed, stretched, stepped on, and abused, they are plagued by shorts and corrosion.

Fortunately, some of the most spectacular causes of fires—alcohol stove flare-ups and explosions from gasoline fumes lurking in the bilges—are becoming less prevalent. This is partly because alcohol is becoming less popular as a cooking fuel, and propane, which is rarely a cause of fire, is now more common. Even among those who stick with alcohol, the traditional pressure stove is passé, having been largely supplanted by the safer and more efficient Origo-type nonpressurized stove.

The increasing awareness among boaters of the consequences of not venting the bilges of gasoline engines has also reduced the number of explosive fires. Unfortunately, however, a belief seems to be taking hold among some boaters that venting is not necessary with fuel-injected gasoline engines. This is not true! While the chances of fume and fuel leakage are diminished with fuel injection, the possibility still exists, and the Coast Guard continues to recommend that bilges be vented before ignition.

While fires caused by engine, transmission, and turbocharger overheating are pretty far down the list in frequency, they move up to the head of the class for fires that occur *while vessels are under way.* Contributing to this is the crew who exacerbates existing conditions—in a nutshell, boaters who immediately open up the engine compartment to find out where all that black smoke is coming from. Opening the hatch provides oxygen to the fire and is the best way to turn what might be an easily extinguished smolder into an abandon ship situation.

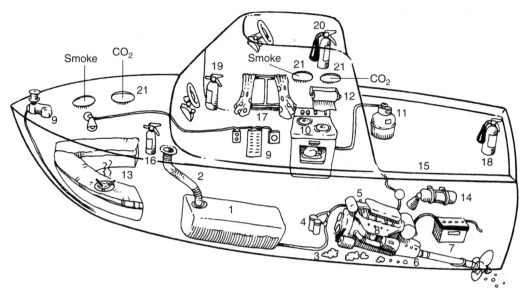

This illustration shows common fire hazards and recommended locations for fire extinguishers.

Fuel and Engine
1. Fuel tank (leaks)
2. Fuel filler line (leaks)
3. Fuel supply line to engine (leaks)
4. Fuel filters (leaks)
5. Carburetors, fuel injectors (leaks)
6. Bilge (accumulated vapors and/or fuel)

Electrical
7. Batteries (sparking from stray object across terminals; explosion due to overcharging)
8. Starter and charging systems (heat from overloaded wiring)
9. House wiring (heat and sparking at poor splices, chafed/broken wiring, overloads)

Galley
10. Stove (fuel flare-ups, oil/grease fires in uncovered fry pans)
11. Propane fuel leaks, malfunctions
12. Curtains, paper towels, trash too close to cooker

Staterooms, Saloon
13. Carelessness with cigarettes, candles
14. Engine compartment: internal, automatic system
15. Outside engine compartment (via fire extinguisher port)
16. All sleeping areas
17. Bulkhead immediately inside companionway
18. Cockpit
19. Helm station(s)
20. Flybridge
21. Crew accommodation and sleeping areas

The proper procedure is to shut down and release the built-in extinguisher. Release valves for vessels with built-in, manually operated fire suppressant systems must be located *outside* engine compartments and machinery spaces. If an installed system isn't aboard, there are plenty of aftermarket choices.

In the absence of an installed fire suppressant system, the boat should at least have a "fire port" to the engine room. This is essentially a small access hatch built into the engine compartment that enables the boat's operator to introduce fire retardant without opening the compartment. While all new vessels without built-in fire extinguishing systems are required to include fire ports, older vessels must be retrofitted. Fire ports are relatively inexpensive, easily installed, and readily available from a number of suppliers, such as West Marine, Boaters World, Fireboy-Xintex, or MarineEast.

Different types of fire extinguishers exist to fight different types of fires. "B"-type fires are those consisting of flammable petroleum products (e.g., engine or cooking fuel). "C"-type fires are electrical in nature. Extinguishers for "B"- and "C"-type fires use carbon dioxide or a dry chemical substance, and most general-purpose extinguishers are marked "B/C." These should be mounted in various locations around the boat where they can be best utilized. "A"-type fires are those involving ordinary combustible materials such as cloth, paper, and wood. By far the least common type of fire aboard recreational boats, these are best extinguished by water or by smothering the fire with a fire-resistant blanket or tarp.

There have been instances of operators of vessels equipped with built-in extinguishers who did not know the valve's location or operation when it became necessary to activate the system, and so lost their boats. Along with knowing and being able to direct passengers to PFD locations, a skipper should know how to deploy the fire suppressant system, including extinguishers, and the location of fuel shut-off valves.

Responding to Fires

No matter how responsible the skipper or owner has been about maintenance and operating procedures, unforeseeable events do occur and the possibility of fire aboard still

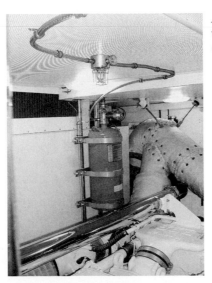

An automatic, built-in fire extinguishing system can sometimes put out a boat fire before you know you have one. (Fireboy-Xintex)

exists. It's then that the preventative steps pay off. The availability of proper and up-to-date fire extinguishers and suppression systems allows options that otherwise might be lacking.

When fire does strike, prioritize the actions that must be taken according to the particular nature of the fire and the situation aboard. The following steps should be taken in the order that a particular emergency demands:

- Attempt to place the boat so flames are downwind from flammables, fuel, or passengers. For example, if the fire is aft, head the bow into the wind so that the flames and smoke are blown away from, not over the boat.

- Determine if the fire is in the engine room. If so, it is likely that keeping the engines running will contribute to the fire, so shutting down the engines may be a better first step, even though this would mean an inability to steer or maintain orientation relative to the wind. In my opinion, if the fire is in the engine room or near the fuel supply, the engines need to be shut down, but the skipper must decide the best course of action based on the immediate situation.

- Turn off fuel shutoffs and battery switches if safely available. If the fire is confined to the engine compartment and shutoffs are located there, any action taken must consider that opening the compartment can feed oxygen to the fire.

- Activate the fire suppressant system, if it is manually operated. If the vessel is equipped with automatic fire suppressant systems, they should have activated by now.

- Determine the whereabouts and condition of all personnel aboard, and order that PFDs be donned.

- Determine the fire's intensity, its location, its immediate effect on the boat and crew, its cause, and whether it appears controllable.

- Communicate to the Coast Guard and surrounding traffic the boat's position and condition. As discussed earlier in this chapter, transmit at least a Pan-Pan message, or Mayday message if there is a possibility of loss of life or the boat sinking. Continue transmitting until communication is established with rescue personnel. An essential part of the transmission—whether the transmission is acknowledged or not—must be the repeated position of the vessel as taken from the GPS and the number of people aboard. A typical transmission would be: "Mayday, Mayday, Mayday; this is the vessel _____. We are experiencing an engine room fire which we have not been able to extinguish. Our position is (latitude/longitude). There are (number of people) aboard." Listen for a response, and if there is no response within 30 seconds, repeat the call. Once communication is established, the Coast Guard may request additional information. The initial call should be as short as possible, primarily giving the name of the vessel, a quick explanation of the emergency, position, and number of people aboard.

- Assign a member of the crew to monitor the VHF, if possible.

Basic Firefighting Tips

BASIC TIPS FOR FIGHTING fires aboard include:

- Use the right type of extinguisher. Don't use water on an electrical fire or on burning oil or fuel. "B," "C," or "B/C" fire extinguishers are the right choice for most fires aboard boats.

- Direct a handheld fire extinguisher at the base of the flames. Using short bursts, sweep the stream from side to side. Keep in mind that most extinguishers have an 8- to 10-second burst time; use bursts effectively. While you're using the extinguisher, have crewmembers bring extra extinguishers from other locations on the boat.

- Make sure the fire is really out after the flames are gone. Fires can continue to smolder and later reignite. In addition, carefully check under nearby floorboards, in lockers, and in other places where a small fire may continue to burn after the main fire has been extinguished. Remove combustibles and "rake" through the area to ensure that there are no remaining hot spots.

- Be particularly careful with bunk and seat cushions. While most new materials supposedly are fire resistant and non-toxic, some older foam-filled cushions have proved extremely flammable, can emit toxic gases, and may continue burning even after being liberally doused with water. If there is any doubt, chuck them overboard and apologize for the possible environmental damage later.

- Identify the vessel's firefighting gear and decide whether fighting the fire has a possibility of success.
- Examine the options of remaining aboard the vessel or abandoning ship. Weigh sea and weather conditions and the availability of lifesaving gear, such as a functional life raft, against the dangers of the fire and the chances of fighting it successfully.

CARBON MONOXIDE POISONING

Late December wouldn't seem like the ideal time to deliver a yacht from Providence, Rhode Island, to Florida. However, the captain had delivered the boat, an older, immaculately maintained twin-diesel trawler, twice before, and she felt comfortable about the trip. Although the temperature hovered just above freezing, the forecast was good, and the boat boasted an efficient cabin heater. She decided on a late afternoon departure and an all-night run down Long Island Sound. The owner and his son, both experienced boaters, would serve as crew, and the captain's two-year-old boat-mutt Bullet would co-captain.

The first leg down Narragansett Bay was uneventful, with the owner and his son switching off at the helm and the skipper napping on the settee. By the time they cleared the bay and began to stretch offshore, both father and son were complaining of dull headaches, which they attributed to minor seasickness and early trip excitement. They went off watch and sacked out. The skipper, feeling a bit queasy herself, took over. After a couple of hours, queasiness was replaced by a feeling of overwhelming exhaustion, which surprised her as she had gotten plenty of rest before and during the trip. She tried to rouse her crew but they were both deeply asleep; even Bullet was lethargic. The skipper decided to enter Fishers Island Sound and run up the Mystic River to a familiar marina and spend the night.

She recalled having a hard time holding a straight course in the sound and, by the time she entered the Mystic, feeling irritated and just wanting to berth the boat and get some sleep. A couple of miles up the river, the channel curves around a large marshy outcrop then straightens out. "The marina I was going to was just around that curve," she later said. "I remember being annoyed that the curve was there and skirted the edge. At the last moment I realized that I wasn't thinking logically."

The trawler nudged into the marsh and ran aground. So be it, she thought, relieved that she would finally be able to get some sleep, and immediately crashed out. She was awakened by a sharp pain in her ankle. It was Bullet sinking his teeth into her.

"I looked down and there was the dog. He had collapsed on the deck but had nipped me hard enough to draw blood," she said. "I jumped up and almost fainted. There appeared to be a heavy weight on my chest, and I had a splitting headache. But I also knew something was terribly wrong, and I think that shot of adrenalin got me going."

She staggered below to find the owner and his son comatose. Unable to wake them, she opened every port in the boat, dragged them out of their bunks, and pummeled them until they came around.

"It was freezing in there, but they got up. We all went on deck. I even dragged Bullet out. Then we all just breathed and breathed and loved the cold air."

She was able to back the boat off, return to the channel, and make it to the marina. There was some damage to the running gear, but a subsequent examination also discovered a break in the generator's exhaust elbow that had allowed fumes to be pumped into the saloon.

"We all had carbon monoxide poisoning and were lucky to be alive," the captain said afterward. "If Bullet hadn't nipped me in the ankle, I don't believe we would've survived. We decided then and there to promote him from mutt to top dog."

Unless you're stumbling along under electric or wind power, your engine, no matter how well tuned, is producing carbon monoxide (CO). And, unfortunately, the happy ending that the trawler's crew experienced was a rarity, for it's truly deadly stuff. In that instance, the CO poisoning resulted from gear failure. In the days of haphazard design and corner-cutting construction, there were instances of death due to faults such as installing ports too close to engine exhausts, or from failing to adequately provide heater or genset ventilation. Thanks to modern design techniques, builder education, and industry monitoring, there have been no reported incidents in recent years concerning new boats with original-equipment installations. However, there have been accidents due to faulty aftermarket installations.

One reason CO is so lethal is that its molecules hitch on to our red blood cells much more effectively than good old oxygen, thereby displacing the oxygen and delivering the wrong stuff to our bodies' internal systems. Those with underlying problems, such as cardiac disease, can have their conditions exacerbated by CO exposure.

Carbon monoxide doesn't necessarily do its insidious work in darkness. The stuff is colorless and odorless, and boaters have succumbed to CO poisoning in the middle of the day while going about their business. And it doesn't even always occur in enclosed spaces; in a relatively recent twist, people, often children, have become ill and some have died from CO poisoning while "teak surfing"—hanging on to the swim platform of cruising and ski boats while being towed at slow speeds.

The area directly behind a boat, even one traveling at speed, constitutes an area of low air pressure that can trap the CO from the exhaust, as well as create the "station wagon effect," which can allow the gas to be vented into the vessel through an open port. Large "greenhouse"-type canvas enclosures, which are often open aft, can also trap CO. The fix is not to hang out on the swim platform or afterdeck at idling speed, especially if there's a following breeze. (In most states it is illegal to ride on the swim platform of a vessel under way.)

If you're skiing, towing a water toy, or wakeboarding, stay at least 20 feet from the boat's stern and definitely not at the level of the exhaust. Often, exhaust gases vent under the surface and then reemerge considerably behind the boat.

All new boats are required to have CO detectors installed. Older boats that did not have detectors as part of their original equipment should have them installed before leaving the dock. Make sure detectors are approved for marine use; the units designed for houses may not survive long in a marine environment. Carbon monoxide detectors should be installed in all sleeping and socializing (saloon) areas. Don't install them in engine rooms, as they'll register too many false alarms. If your CO detectors are powered by a self-contained 9-volt battery (as opposed to being hardwired into the house DC system), make battery replacement a part of your annual maintenance routine for the boat.

Recognizing and Treating CO Poisoning

The initial signs of carbon monoxide poisoning are nonspecific and often mistaken for fatigue and/or signs of a cold or virus. A fast heart rate, a pounding or "runaway" pulse, and rapid breathing are more specific early warning signs. The classic signs of advanced CO poisoning, however—cyanosis (a bluish discoloration of the skin and mucous membranes), retinal hemorrhage (hemorrhage within the innermost membrane covering the eyeball, resulting in a "bloody red" appearance), and cherry-red lips—are rarely seen except in severe, and often moribund, cases.

The following symptoms, in order of most frequency, can be indicators of CO poisoning. If two or more are present along with the possibility of CO generation (engines, gensets, heaters), CO poisoning should be suspected.

1. Headache
2. Dizziness
3. Irritability

4. Confusion/memory loss

5. Disorientation

6. Nausea and vomiting

7. Abnormal reflexes

8. Difficulty with coordination

9. Difficulty in breathing

10. Chest pain

Immediate treatment is straightforward. Get the victim into fresh air, discontinue whatever appears to be generating the CO, and keep the victim warm and comfortable. If symptoms appear severe or persist, get to port immediately or get on the VHF and call for help. It is important to continually monitor the victim's breathing and heart rate to determine if they are returning to normal.

GROUNDING

The brand-new 18-foot Bayliner was as much out of its element as a seagull on a desert dune. Perched like a lonely sentinel at least 15 feet from the high-tide line and visible for miles on the flat expanse of a New Jersey beach, it was a sad sight indeed. A small crowd surrounded the boat. Some were onlookers; others were scooping muck out of the swamped craft while a few were digging a trench to the water preparatory to hauling the boat around and pushing it back out so it could be retrieved by a waiting towboat.

Delightful weather and a calm day probably encouraged the boat's skipper to run somewhat closer to the shore than he normally would have. From his offshore vantage point, the slight swell running in appeared harmless. But as he ran slowly along the coast the swell that was gently lifting his boat—and bringing it ever closer to the shore—gradually became higher and steeper.

Swells do that. It's called wave dynamics. As a wave approaches shallower water, it can become steeper prior to breaking. An observer on shore will see the end result of the process— the breaking wave. The offshore boater, however, is viewing the back end of the wave. He is not in a position to see its forward curl—which can become a breaker—until it's too late.

Waves break where the water shallows. Of course this usually occurs close to the shore, but it is also common for shallows to extend far from shore, and for a bar to create a shallow far from shore with a stretch of relatively deep water in between. This makes it possible for a boater to be running close to shore in deep, calm water, and suddenly find himself shoreward of breaking seas. That's what happened to the Bayliner. One moment its skipper thought he was safely off the beach; the next moment he looked seaward and spotted the rising breaker that broached him, lifted the boat, spun it around, and swamped it. Succeeding swells took it ashore. He was also unlucky enough to pick the last hour of the high tide, ensuring a lofty perch for the next few hours.

Most boaters who find themselves on the beach are there because they were operating too close to shore. Whenever running close inshore, be aware of changes in wave patterns and the feel of the boat. Although a beach line could look fairly straight when running parallel to it, the underwater configuration isn't necessarily straight. Fingers of shoal often extend far offshore, and there can be the stubs of old jetties or pilings and even hulks of forgotten wrecks. A few years ago, a Maine boater hit an object that turned out to be the remnants of the boiler of a nineteenth-century steamer. He stated that he noticed "swirls" in the water ahead of him, but his depth sounder showed relatively deep water. Believing that he was far enough off the beach, he continued over the disturbed area, assuming that it was a tidal rip. He not only was mistaken, but the obstruction was noted on the charts.

A change in a wave pattern close inshore could be indicative of a shoal area or an obstruction. Be particularly aware of ripples or small patches of chop that are not obviously windblown. Know the tidal picture. A safe distance off when the tide is high could be perilous at low tide.

Keep a light touch on the helm; boats react differently in shoaling water, and if you're paying close attention, you might notice a different "feel" to the boat. Some cruisers will squat in the stern upon entering shoal water; others tend to turn away from shoal areas. Old-time Mississippi or Missouri River pilots swear their boats will steer themselves away from shoaling bends on those rivers. However, it's not advisable for the pleasure boater to assume that his or her boat will keep itself off the beach. You need to be more proactive.

Grounding Due to Engine Failure

When a vessel loses power when running near shore with an onshore breeze or current, the rule is to immediately get the hook down in the hope that it will set before the boat is driven ashore.

However, due to a steeply shelving beach, poor holding, severe surf conditions, or insufficient ground tackle, the anchor might not set before the boat is beached. When it appears unlikely that the anchor will set in time to keep the boat from being set ashore, deploying the anchor may cause more harm than good. If the anchor entirely fails to hold, the boat will likely turn sideways to the waves, resulting in a possible broach or swamping. If the anchor manages to hold only poorly and drags, the boat may approach the shore stern-first, in which case the running gear will likely be damaged as soon as the boat makes contact with the bottom, and the boat will be turned broadside to the beach by the first wave, resulting, again, in a broach or swamping.

If, in the skipper's opinion, it doesn't appear that an anchor will hold, make an effort to keep the stern to the seas and allow the boat to ride in bow-first in order to minimize personal injury and physical damage. Factors that need be considered are the quality, type, and condition of the ground tackle; the severity of the weather; and the distance of the breaking surf line from the beach. A disabled boat equipped with light ground tackle being affected by a severe onshore breeze approaching strong breakers will probably not anchor successfully.

In such a situation a drogue—either a commercially available one carried aboard, or one contrived from materials on hand—can help keep the stern to the seas and the bow pointing downwind. (See Chapter 3 for how to rig a drogue.) The more material streamed aft, the more effective the drogue will be, so the larger the boat, the larger the drogue must be. I was once able to beach in near-storm conditions—with minimal additional damage—a disabled 45-foot sportfisherman by floating a spare 60-pound anchor buoyed with life vests and fenders astern. If a long line with its bight isn't practical, a shorter line attached to a bridle, also with floatable material attached, might work.

Stabilizing the Boat

Once the boat is beached, attempt to either move it away from the breaking surf or stabilize it in the bow-forward position. With very small craft, it may be possible to place fenders beneath the hull to assist in rolling the boat up the beach. Boats have been successfully moved out of danger by using the effects of the tide or surf, supplemented by lines to a fixed point above the high-tide line, to ride it farther up the beach. Lines should be run from bow cleats to a tree or other fixed point. If nothing solid is in reach of your lines, an anchor may be buried in the ground above the high-water line. Make the bow line as tight as possible, and retighten it as the boat is moved either manually or by surf action up the beach. Use any available mechanical aids, such as blocks, winches, or an anchor windlass to tighten the line. If none of these are available, you can improvise mechanical advantage by tying a loop in the line between the boat and the anchoring point, and using this as a single-point pulley.

For deep-keeled powerboats, like some trawlers, that might not stand upright on a beach, it may be tempting to try to prop them upright rather than allow them to remain on their sides. I wouldn't attempt it. Even if you could find suitable long, strong poles to use (and if your boat

Pulling a grounded boat out of harm's way from damaging waves. Failing a block and tackle, a bowline, shackle, or ring tied into the towline will provide some mechanical advantage and allow you to pull downhill rather than up. Use fenders or logs as rollers beneath the hull.

Pulling a boat up a ramp on fenders. How in the world am I going to haul this heavy dinghy and motor out all by myself? The same principles that are employed during a grounding will work just fine.

These fenders should do the trick.

Say, didn't they build the pyramids this way?

Two fenders are better than one, and if the hull were longer, three or more would be better still.

Up and out. Just remember to have the fenders support the heaviest part of the hull.

Easing a boat down a ramp on fenders. Fender-rollers make it easy to launch the dinghy as well.

Placing a loop in the painter line helps ease the boat back down the ramp.

Doubling the loop in the line allows for an additional mechanical advantage, either in lowering the boat or hauling it farther out.

is a trawler, these would have to be at least four-by-fours, if not I-beams), the prospects of making the arrangement stable with the boat still subject to tide and waves are not good, while the prospects of it tipping over, possibly on yourself, are excellent.

Hard Groundings

There is an interesting formation off the northeast end of Connecticut's Fishers Island Sound called Seal Rocks, so named because the critters hang out there in the winter months. Occasionally, how-ever, the wildlife gets scared away by the approach of a boat that proceeds to mount the rock. In one incident, a delivery crew returning north aboard a fast 72-footer grounded on Seal Rocks. The skip-per then turned bad seamanship into a near disaster. Having trashed only one prop, shaft, and strut, he used the other to back off—which he did successfully, only to have the stern fill with tons of water, which entered through the big hole where his starboard running gear used to be. The boat didn't sink, but only because of the quick response of three towboats and their heavy-duty pumps.

A "hard grounding" occurs when you run your vessel aground under power. You should back off following a grounding only when staying in place will put the boat or crew in further danger—when the boat is being pounded by surf or seas, for instance.

With any type of grounding, from a barely perceptible "thump" to an actual rock climb, it's imperative to tie up or stop the boat, go below, and carefully check for leaks, paying particular attention to the area around stuffing boxes and seacocks. Unless the vessel is a heavy keeled trawler or sailboat, the odds are there will be some damage. Often, the damage will be a nicked prop, bent strut, or damaged shaft that might not be apparent from inside the boat, but that might manifest itself if you get under way again. All too often a relatively minor and easily repaired problem is exacerbated by continuing to run the boat. Any powerboat with exposed shafts, rudders, or props that experiences any level of grounding must immediately stop and shut the engines down (if safe) and inspect the running gear for damage and the bilge for leaks.

In the event of a hard grounding:

1. Determine if there are any injuries and administer first aid to serious ones.
2. Jot down your exact position.
3. See if the boat is taking on water and ascertain its structural condition.
4. Report the situation and position to a commercial tower and/or the Coast Guard.
5. Determine the state of the tide. If the boat took the bottom on a falling tide, it'll be higher and harder aground shortly. If the tide is rising, the boat can float free, which might not be desirable. Keep in mind that what appears to be a small leak when the boat is relatively high may become more serious as the tide rises.
6. Attempt to place an anchor in deep water if help isn't immediately available. The anchor is best set from the bow, especially with smaller boats, to avoid the possibility of swamping or water coming aboard from aft as it pulls off. (See Chapter 6 for details on placing an anchor from a dinghy.) If the boat floats free for any reason, the anchor will keep you from being set right back on the rocks.

9

Keeping Water on the Outside

A few years ago my daughter and I were cruising on Long Island Sound aboard a brand-new 34-foot twin-engine cruiser lent to us by a boatbuilder. The trip was part long-term boat test, part cruising story, and a bit of dad trying to convince kid that life on the water also existed by means other than wind power. It was a theory that was immediately put to the test.

Right after we left Block Island for Martha's Vineyard, a nasty chop raised by a stiff southeasterly convinced me that Newport—downwind and downsea—would really be nicer to visit. But shortly after we turned, and while I was below punching in waypoints, with my daughter at the upper station, the boat fell off plane. I hollered up to add power.

She replied that the throttles were firewalled and that the boat was beginning to feel funny. Translate that to wallow—enough for her to get down from the flybridge, fearful of the weight aloft, and for me to head for the bilges—which resembled a full washing machine complete with engine belts churning up water like berserk agitators. At that point, one engine died. As I grabbed the VHF, I noticed that the bilge pump light was serenely off—and stayed that way when I threw it on manual.

A couple of anxiety-ridden hours later, followed by a flotilla that included a Coast Guard cutter, a hopeful commercial tower, and the Block Island ferry, we limped into the aptly named Point Judith Harbor of Refuge. After two hours of a 2 ½-inch gasoline-engine-powered pump going full-bore, the boat was dewatered. The problem? A faulty weld on one engine's raw-water intake elbows failed and had us pumping cooling water directly into the bilge. Fortunately, that was the engine that drowned out. If the other one had gone, we would have been left treading water. So, what happened to the bilge pump? The builder (who shall remain nameless and who will never, never run wires that way again) had strung unprotected pump wiring—joined by nonwaterproof butt connectors—along a stringer at the lowest point in the bilge. As soon as wires got wet they shorted out. Duhh!

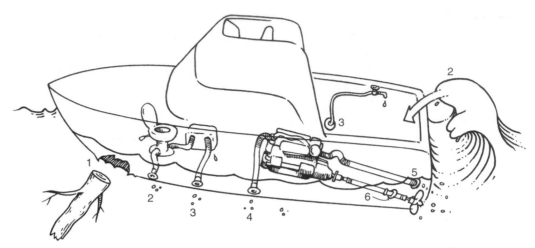

Common sources of water incursion include: hole below the waterline due to collision or grounding damage (1); swamping of the cockpit by a wave over the transom (2); any through-hull fitting, including head intake and overboard discharge and auxiliary washdown pump (3); raw-water intake for engine cooling (4); below-the-waterline exhaust (5); and shaft log and Cutless bearing (6).

Outside of the drama of it all, that's the type of water incursion that's highly preventable—and quite common. A great percentage of water incursions can be dealt with from within—by stopping the engines when there's a cooling system failure or closing a valve. Taste the water (unless you're on a lake); sometimes it can be as simple as a freshwater tank rupturing or (ugh) a holding tank (then, don't taste).

There are procedures to follow when water incursion occurs while under way, but prevention—which essentially is an intimate knowledge of your boat—is a lot less expensive and stressful. Unless you slam into something very hard and open up a whole new entrance for water to get in, there are a finite number of places where water can get in, and most of those areas are amenable to preventive maintenance.

PARTS THAT LEAK

The failure of seacocks, through-hull fittings, or the hosing leading to them can result in a potentially catastrophic water incursion. The simplest and most effective preventive measures consist of examining them at least once a month during the season, and overhauling them annually during the haulout.

During your monthly inspection, open and close the seacocks to make sure they move freely, and eyeball and handle all through-hull fittings; if they're wet or you feel movement, look closer. Some wetness may be due to condensation, but that's easy to rule out. If there is "condensation" on one fitting and none on an adjacent one, be suspicious. If the boat is in salt water, a taste test settles the matter, as condensation isn't salty. Since condensation takes some time to form, wipe the fitting dry. If it's wet again shortly thereafter, you've got a leaking fitting.

Make a map or diagram of the location and the open/close position of all the sea-cocks in your boat. Keep one copy with the ship's papers, and another laminated copy posted where it can be easily spotted if you're not aboard.

Composite valves—those made of plastic or various resin-infused compounds—concern me. If you don't operate them for a while the handles freeze in place (even though the internals are still viable). Bear down on them and they break. That's the time to replace the whole thing with a proper metal one. Boats used in fresh water may be equipped with through-hulls and seacocks made of brass or a mix of brass and bronze construction. These will inevitably corrode in salt water, however, so solid bronze sea-cocks and through-hulls are required for salt water use. Buy seacocks in established chandleries and look for brand names like Groco and Perko.

It is highly unusual for the heavily built handle of a bronze marine seacock to break. If it does, it is still possible to see by the broken piece of handle whether the valve is in the open or closed position, unless the break is at the extreme base. Some seacock handles, however, are not integral to the base of the valve and can be removed. The handles are notched so they can be placed over a square nut that actually works the valve. This type of seacock is typically placed in a restricted space where its handle in the open or closed position might interfere with a hatch or deck board. In such instances, it cannot be easily determined whether the valve is open or closed unless the handle is installed. When removed the handle must be connected to the valve by a small chain or line so it can be immediately installed.

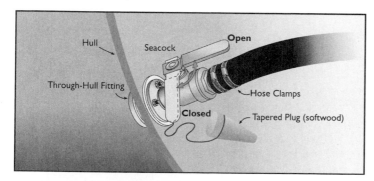

Ball-type seacock in open and closed positions. When it's closed, the handle lies "across" the flow of water. When open, it points the way. (Joe Comeau)

Note the single hose clamp on this recently installed seacock. Two clamps are preferred (and safer).

Seacocks versus Gate Valves

WHILE ALL NEW BOATS are equipped with sea-cocks, many older boats were built or retro-fitted with gate valves. Proper seacocks are the only acceptable choice. If your boat has gate valves, replace them.

The position of the gate valve handle gives no indication as to whether it's open or closed, whereas you can always tell at a glance with a seacock. When the seacock handle is in line with the hose, pipe, or fitting to which it's connected, that indicates that the liquid can flow straight through, i.e., it's open. When the handle is at right angles to the hose, it's like a wall across the flow; therefore, it's closed.

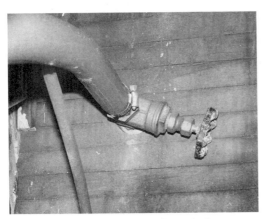

This gate valve has no place aboard a boat.

All through-hulls should be equipped with a ball-type seacock.

Hoses are also prime culprits in water incursion incidents. They get old, deteriorate, and fail. Head hoses seem to be the most susceptible, possibly because they are inspected rarely due to their unwholesome location.

Feel a hose. It shouldn't be wet. (See the previous discussion on condensation.) If the hose takes a sharp bend, especially where it first leaves a fitting, that's a dead giveaway that the hose will fail—it is just a matter of when. Ribbed automotive hoses are anathema on a boat. They are lined with steel wire, which will rust, break, and destroy the hose from the inside. Marine-grade hosing, marked as such and purchased from a reliable marine sup-plier, is the only way to go.

The Cutless bearing is a ribbed rubber or neoprene sleeve in the end of the through-hull fitting or strut that supports the propeller shaft. This bearing is designed to allow a small amount of water through to cool and lubricate the shaft. Even when the bearing is worn, it is rarely the direct cause of problematical water incursions, although they have been known to happen. However, a worn Cutless bearing can cause excessive play in the shaft, resulting in vibration and strain upon the shaft/transmission coupling and/or excessive wear, which can lead to serious leaking of the stuffing box. And if that happens, you *do* have a problematic water incursion incident.

When the boat is hauled, a simple test for Cutless bearing wear is to see if there is play in the shaft when you heave on it. Some minute movement is acceptable as it allows enough water through to lubricate the bearing. Excessive movement, or if you are able to move the shaft in a circular or "wobbling" motion, indicates bearing wear. Replace it.

HANDLING A WATER INCURSION

The old sailor's tale of the world's best bilge pump being a scared man with a bucket doesn't quite hold water (so to speak). On today's powerboats with their complex systems and creative use of space, there often just isn't enough room to dip a good-sized galvanized bucket (which, as we've discussed repeatedly, should be aboard anyway as standard equipment) until the water gets into the wide-open spaces of the cabin sole. At that point removing the water will be an exercise in futility and your primary concern will be getting the life raft launched. One sad truth is that in the event of a catastrophic water incursion, standard electric bilge pumps will, most likely, not save the boat.

Water incursions from ruptured hoses and failed fittings can be intense. Depending on how far below the waterline and the diameter of the hose or the fitting, the water can come in with surprising pressure. There have been occasions in which personnel attempting to deal with such an influx were overwhelmed by what they perceived as an unmanageable flood and abandoned the job, and the boat, when subsequent investigation determined that more effort would have stemmed the tide.

Since most water incursions are due to failed through-hulls, seacocks, and hoses, you should keep a variety of tapered softwood plugs aboard, along with a hammer to pound them into place. (Plugs are available at most chandleries.) When it's time to place the plug, it should be hammered in with force. Softwood plugs will not damage or crack the hull.

Stow wood plugs of various sizes aboard to plug any failed through-hulls. For immediate access, you can wire one plug of the appropriate size next to every through-hull.

Plugs Are No Guarantee

A DELIVERY CAPTAIN I know learned the hard way that just having wood plugs aboard doesn't guarantee that you can stop a leak due to a failed through-hull. While making a repair in a tight bilge while under way, he inadvertently snapped a composite fitting off a few inches above its through-hull connection, and the water shot through with force. When he attempted to pound a wooden plug into the break, the fitting split lengthwise—letting in just as much water, only moving in a different direction. He had to hacksaw the fitting until it was flush with the hull before he could achieve a tight seal with the plug.

It sounds simple, but in practice, it may not be such an easy fix. Due to the configuration of the bilge, intruding wiring and plumbing, and the various types of seacocks and through-hulls in service, it might be difficult to efficiently force in a plug. Articulations in hosing; old, corroded plumbing; stem-type through-hull/seacock combinations; and composite seacocks may not offer a clean hole to plug. A hacksaw, wire cutter, possibly a bolt cutter, and two or three sharp knives—at least one with a serrated blade—with strong cutting edges should be available to cut away, if necessary, hosing or other material that can prevent the plug from being driven home.

Often, an influx from a broken hose can be dealt with by bypassing the break and simply following the hosing to the seacock and closing it. There have been instances of panicked crew trying to repair the hose, when bypassing the break would have easily solved the problem.

Tapered wooden plugs will rarely stem the flow of a broken hose, and it is usually a waste of time to attempt it. Broken hosing or corroded clamps and fittings will usually prevent the plug from being properly installed, and sometimes the influx of water must be ignored while the surface is prepared. It might be necessary to completely remove a corroded or broken fitting or hose before the plug can be inserted properly. Broken hoses can rarely be cleanly removed with just a sharp knife. Many hoses are metal-ribbed, and a powerful wire cutter or possibly a bolt cutter must be used to remove them.

Again, the actions described here are performed amidst a daunting influx of water. It may sound trite, but on more than one occasion I have been in such a situation and know that the proper mental attitude is important. As long as the bilges are accessible and action is being taken to stop the leak, the person assigned to that task must ignore the influx and focus on the job at hand. Keep at it until you succeed, as long as the boat remains afloat.

The coupling between the transmission and the prop shaft is among the most vulnerable in a boat's drivetrain. The forces upon that connection when the boat is put into gear are enormous and can act to loosen any nut-bolt fastening. The bolts, therefore, should be safety wired as an added precaution. Nevertheless, possibly because of the coupling's hard-to-reach location on many boats that makes inspection difficult, vibration—aided

Get Creative

PARTS AND MATERIALS INTENDED for totally different purposes can often serve to jury-rig repairs. In similar recent incidents aboard two different boats, packing-type stuffing boxes separated, one due to failure of the packing, the other because the set nuts came loose. One of the crews couldn't stem the influx of water and had to run the sinking boat ashore. On the other boat, the skipper cut a piece of spare cooling hose lengthwise, rolled and jammed it over the shaft, and secured it with hose clamps and duct tape. This curtailed most of the leak and enabled the boat to proceed to port on the other engine.

---

by electrolysis and corrosion—may do its work, causing the coupling to separate. When the boat is put into forward gear and the coupling separates, the only result is that the boat loses power; there will be no water incursion. However, if the coupling separates when the engine is placed in reverse, the prop can pull the shaft completely through the stern gland. The water incursion through the shaft aperture will then be intense and, in most cases, unmanageable due to the location and the amount of water coming through a large hole in the hull.

A saving grace is that way is immediately lost but the engine continues running, so an alert crew will immediately know why the boat stopped and know exactly where to look for the incursion. If they react quickly, the crew can attempt to stem the flow by wrapping a blanket or sheet around the blunt end of a boathook and jamming it into the aperture. There have also been instances where fothering, described below, has worked to an extent, but this can be highly problematic, due to the under-hull location of the aperture and the presence of struts and rudders as well as the boat's chine or deadrise.

USING THE ENGINE AS A BILGE PUMP

An aquatic version of an urban legend is that in the event of a massive water incursion the engine intake cooling hose can be used to drain the bilge. Theoretically the seacock can be closed, and the cooling hose removed or cut and then placed in the bilge where the engine's raw-water pump will remove the bilge water to cool the engine. This procedure undoubtedly saved many wooden, deep-bilged fishing and commercial boats years ago. In today's modern, relatively shallow-bilged pleasure boats, however, the hose will probably not be able to suck sufficient water to prevent the engine from overheating. Other impediments may be that the pump will lose its prime when you disconnect the intake hose, or the intake will become clogged with debris washed out of the bilges—especially if the boat is in a seaway.

Having said that, if it appears that the boat is sinking and the engine is still running and there is no other way to remove water, you might want to give it a try. However, with preparation and minimal effort, a more efficient system can be devised to make use of the engine's water pump.

In an emergency, you can remove the engine's raw-water intake hose from the through-hull (close the seacock first!), place the end in the bilge, and use the water pump to remove the water. (Joe Comeau)

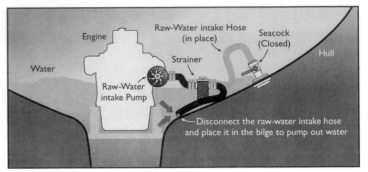

Install a T-fitting placed in-line on the water intake hose, between the seacock and the engine. From the base of the T, which faces the bilge, attach a short section of hose. Install a seacock there and then another section of hose, down to the bilge. Place a raw-water strainer at its end, and secure it in the bottom of the bilge. (A Y-diverter may be used in place of the T-fitting and seacock.)

In the event of a serious leak, the through-hull seacock is closed and the bilge hose seacock is opened. The engine will then take its cooling water from the bilge. It is imperative that the level of bilge water and the engine's temperature be closely monitored while it is pumping the bilge. If the pump actually succeeds in lowering the leak, you want to be ready to switch over to the cooling water before you run the pump dry.

FOTHERING

Worst-case scenarios often call for last resort remedies. Striking an obstacle—or another boat—at speed while under way qualifies on both counts. If the boat has been holed, help is not immediately available, and other methods to remove water are insufficient, fothering may be your best, last resort.

Fothering has been used almost since the time men first went to sea. Originally, it was a sail tied at four corners and led under the hull from the bow aft (or from stern forward) until it covered the hole and water pressure held it in place. While most powerboats don't have sails handy (trawlers with steadying sails have an advantage here), the following have all been used successfully: tarps, bimini tops, cockpit covers, aft-deck covers, blankets, bed linens, and seat covers. Use whatever is available.

Used in this way, the fothering material is called a collision mat. Long, stout lines are bent to each corner of the material; bend over the corners of material of lighter weight such as blankets to give added support before piercing it for the lines. The mat is then lowered over the bow (or stern) and walked aft or forward by the ropes with crew on either side. When the mat is pulled over the hole in the hull, the incoming water pressure should pull it across the hole and hold it in place. Protrusions from the hull or anything that prevents the mat from being in direct contact with the hull could render the mat ineffective. The chines on a powerboat, for example, could hold the mat clear of the hull.

You can significantly slow the inflow of water through a hole in the hull by *fothering* it—covering it with a tarp, cushion, or similar material.

I know of an incident in which a boat struck a "deadman"—a log or pole floating vertically in the water with the top barely awash. The boat was holed below the waterline on the starboard side, 2 feet from the chine, which prevented the mat from covering the hole. The crew on the starboard side eased their lines while those on the port side pulled theirs in. The mat then cleared the chine and was able to adhere to the hole, significantly slowing the leak.

GLOP

As part of their emergency kits, many boaters carry a supply of "underwater epoxy" or waterproof structural adhesive, assuming they can use it to stop leaks. Possibly, with small leaks, when properly applied and given time to set, these materials will work. In the event of a large leak or water incursion, however, depending on waterproof epoxies or adhesives can be dangerous as a forceful incursion of water can wash the material away. Even if the material can be applied to a patch—a piece of wood, for instance—the patch must still be held in place until the adhesive sets. And the length of time to set, even for the most efficient of epoxies and adhesives, dramatically increases when wet.

Having said that, an underwater structural adhesive did save the day when an express cruiser at planing speed hit a rocky outcrop. The collision pushed a strut, complete with its backing plate, through the hull. The quick-thinking crew forced the protruding strut back through the hull and covered the resulting hole with a bunk board roughly cut to fit and liberally smeared with 3M 5200 structural adhesive. They hacksawed another bunk board into strips, which they used as wedges to secure the patch in place. The resulting repair combined with vigorous pumping enabled the boat to stay afloat until help arrived. In that instance, the 5200 served a valuable purpose, once the board was held securely in place and the adhesive was given time to set.

10
Abandoning Ship

I belong to a very exclusive club, and I'm not saying that with any particular pride. The club is comprised of those who've had to resort to life rafts to keep from joining their vessels in a watery grave. I would have preferred not to join this club, and wouldn't have had to if I had not done something, or a number of things, particularly stupid. Statistics show that I'm not alone. The great majority of members usually end up in the drink as the end result of a progression of sins, both of commission and omission.

Sure, sinking situations do arise occasionally due to no fault of the victim—the semi-submerged container, a microburst in the midst of a severe squall, the totally inexplicable equipment failure. But those are relatively rare. Upon post-rescue review, most members clearly see the progression of incidents and/or ill-planned or ill-advised procedures that led to their inevitable downfall. And it's usually a progression; there are few things that have such disastrous domino effects as poor nautical judgment.

In my case, I was in such a hurry to jump offshore and bring an ancient, decrepit wooden cruiser from Ft. Lauderdale to New York that I didn't properly inspect the boat or see to it that necessary maintenance was performed. The reason for rushing? I wanted to bring an equally ancient and decrepit ten-person life raft, which I had picked up cheap at the annual Dania Marine Flea Market and which hadn't been serviced in at least fifteen years, to New York, where I had cut a deal to get it repacked and sold at a healthy profit. Other than that, I thought having a life raft aboard was sissy stuff that took up important sunning space. Hey, I was 23 years old and knew everything worth knowing.

The boat broke up in a severe gale off Brigantine, New Jersey, and suddenly that old raft was manna from heaven. We tailed the painter to a cleat, tossed it overboard, and prepared to jump in.

But the thing didn't open. It just floated there like a big blob of wet yellow canvas. But at least it was floating, and the boat definitely wasn't going to continue doing that for much longer. Just before we launched ourselves off the boat, a big wave picked up the raft and slammed it against the boat. When it rebounded, the painter snapped and the raft began to inflate at the same time. My two buddies and I dove into that raft so fast we didn't even get our feet wet—until it promptly filled to the brim. But it still floated, and a couple of hours later, half-drowned, we washed up on Brigantine beach.

In the years—many years—since washing up on Brigantine beach in a life boat, I've acquired a healthy interest in life rafts. From reading the literature and questioning Coast Guard and other rescue specialists, I've come to a few conclusions on key questions. This common one, for instance: When should a life raft be aboard?

The answer is: all the time, if the boat regularly goes to sea—and that includes lakes, bays, sounds . . . any body of water large enough that you may not be able to swim ashore. To the best of my knowledge, people who drown in relatively protected waters look pretty much the same as those who do so offshore. It pays to keep in mind that the most *uncommon* cause of vessels in distress is violent weather far from land. Boats sink or need to be abandoned due to myriad unexpected conditions—including fires, explosions, and maniacal spouses—that can occur on any body of water.

LIFE RAFT SELECTION

This brings us to another frequently asked question about life rafts: What type of raft should a particular vessel carry?

Life rafts range from orange, usually oval-shaped floating platforms with dangle-your-feet-in-the-water hang-on straps, through single-tube devices called "coastal" life rafts, to the traditional double-tubed, canopy-protected "offshore" life rafts. They are further differentiated in equipment-carrying capacity, from basic keep-you-barely-alive essentials, through the enough-gear-to-satisfy-a-pack-of-ravenous-Boy-Scouts categories. Prices, of course, vary accordingly.

Know what, if any, survival equipment is included in your life raft. In addition, it pays to have a ditch bag containing additional food, water, and communication devices ready to accompany you aboard the raft. If it is necessary to launch a flare, make sure you ignite it *outside* the raft. (Winslow)

I equate the floating platform types to the minuscule "doughnuts" that auto manufacturers try to pass off as spare tires—somebody's trying to save a buck. While the auto spare will merely make you look silly as you roll down the road, dangling your footsies tantalizingly in front of the local shark population goes beyond silly.

"Coastal" life rafts are aimed at the majority of boaters, who don't regularly contemplate ocean crossings. This makes me think of the not-so-rare newspaper story of the guy who goes a couple of miles out for a day of bottom fishing, has an engine failure (fire, flood, you name it), and come morning finds himself surrounded by your basic 360-degree horizon and nothing else. Because we heard of it, that particular boater survived to tell the tale. The questions being: What is coastal and where does coastal end and offshore begin? And why, when I am floating in coastal waters without a boat, am I less in danger than when I am floating in offshore waters?

The idea behind "coastal" life rafts is that if you're in trouble in near-shore waters, you have more of a chance of being found quickly, and, therefore, you don't need a substantial life raft. Me? I prefer not to take that bet. When I'm in a jam, I want to deploy the best and most substantial life raft available.

Life rafts are rated according to the number of people they are designed to carry. The number of passengers and crew aboard your boat should be limited to the life raft's rated capacity. If you want to carry more passengers, get a bigger raft or buy or rent a second one.

Although raft designs and features vary, the following are my preferences:

- The raft should have ballast pockets or water bladders to provide stability in high sea conditions.
- A canopy and an insulated floor are needed to provide protection from the elements.
- The life raft's boarding mechanism (i.e., ladder, grab straps, or inflated platform) should be appropriate to the least physically able of the boat's passengers.
- The life raft should be encircled by a well-backed and secured grab line.

Boarding Mechanisms

Some life rafts have inflatable boarding platforms that may be semi-submerged or that float on the surface. Others have two- or three-rung ladders made from either a rigid or a flexible material. And some have nothing but a tab above the rim for you to grab and pull yourself up and in.

I think ladders and grab straps are next to useless. The ability to use them successfully depends to a large extent on your physical condition. Aside from the fact that many of us are out of shape in the best of circumstances, consider the conditions of a sinking boat. You may be injured, hypothermic, in shock—certainly scared and confused, and, possibly, closer to panicky. Even if you're fit and uninjured, what about your passengers? Never mind the supposed extra strength that adrenaline is supposed to provide when you're frightened—you're in a life-threatening situation under highly adverse conditions, and this is not the time to see if you can do a pull-up for the first time since you were 18.

Boarding a life raft is often undertaken in extremely adverse circumstances. Prior to purchasing a life raft, make sure its boarding system is sufficient for the least able of those who might use it. (Winslow)

(You're also wearing a life vest, which can be pretty restrictive.) For all these reasons, I prefer a raft with an inflated, semi-submerged boarding platform with proper handholds. See them inflated at the boat shows and talk to the reps before you make a decision.

On the other hand, if you're 23 and dumb, all this stuff is moot anyway. Just get out there and do it—but don't expect to be pontificating about it 30 years later. You might not be as lucky as I was.

Outfitting a Life Raft

EVERY LIFE RAFT NEEDS a survival kit and a selection of ancillary gear, including the following:

- Drogue or sea anchor
- Emergency Position Indicating Radio Beacon (EPIRB)
- Various visual and sound signaling devices such as an up-to-date flare kit including day and night pyrotechnics, a whistle, an air horn, and dye markers
- Folding knife
- Rainwater collector
- Painter permanently attached to a reinforced bow fitting
- Paddle
- Sealed containers of water and emergency rations (updated and replaced during regular inspections)
- Manufacturer-supplied repair kit

DEPLOYING THE LIFE RAFT

Lives have needlessly been lost after the life raft has been launched. Often, this is due to one of two problems. Either the raft did not open after it was deployed or, upon its opening, the victim was unable to board the raft.

Inflatable life rafts are equipped with a long section of line that goes by two names. Before you toss the package overboard, you tie this *static line* to a cleat. When it's in the water, you pull on the static line to trigger the inflation mechanism; when the raft is inflated, the line magically becomes a *painter*.

A static line may be 30–100 feet long, and it takes a good healthy yank to get the raft to inflate. In some cases where lives were lost due to a raft not inflating, subsequent inspection found coils of line still stowed in the pocket. The victims simply hadn't hauled it all out and yanked hard enough. Due entirely to my own ignorance, I was in precisely that same predicament that night off New Jersey, and if that wave hadn't picked up the raft and yanked its painter free, I wouldn't be pontificating now.

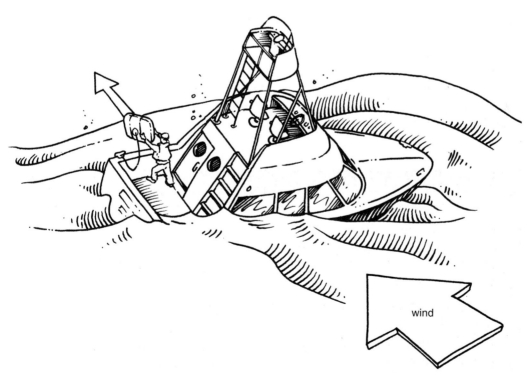

When the time comes to deploy the life raft, tie off the static line to a cleat or other secure fitting on the boat. Throw the raft to the downwind (lee) side of the boat, pull the static line all the way out, and give it a sharp yank to begin the inflation process.

The static line needs to be attached to a substantial piece of the boat's structure before the raft is tossed overboard. *All* of the available line must then be pulled free from its stowage pouch and given a substantial yank—hard enough to rip through the retaining fabric. It's made that way to prevent accidental inflation.

Here's the drill:

- *Do not* inflate the life raft until it is launched.
- Secure the inflatable life raft's static line to a substantial structural part of the boat, such as a cleat, radar arch, or windlass base. Do not use lifeline stanchions or canvas support struts, as they can pull loose.
- Toss the uninflated life raft overboard from the boat's leeward quadrant—the downwind/-sea part of the vessel.
- Once the life raft is launched, haul in the static line and give it a good, hard yank to inflate it. If it doesn't inflate, yank harder!

ABANDONING SHIP

OK, the time has come. Disaster has struck your boat, and you've determined that it can't be saved—or that any further attempt to save it would expose passengers and crew to a greater probability of danger than abandoning ship would.

Unfortunately, unlike the relatively straightforward task of launching the life raft, there's no consistent procedure to follow for the larger abandon-ship process, since a lot will depend on the particular nature of the emergency and the number and capabilities of the boat's crew. For instance, if there are enough well-trained personnel aboard, the skipper can assign responsibilities that will ensure that various tasks are performed simultaneously—launching the raft, transmitting the Mayday, and so on. With a smaller crew, or passengers who are unable to perform such functions, more responsibility will fall on those able to carry on such tasks—possibly the skipper alone. In that case, deciding upon the order in which various actions must be taken will depend upon the situation.

For example, if the boat is on fire, the captain must consider where the inflated raft will be in relation to the burning boat when it is launched. It must be launched to leeward of the mother ship, but with flames and smoke also being blown to leeward, it might not be wise to secure the raft to the vessel being abandoned. Since, in this case, the life raft must be boarded and freed *immediately* upon deployment, any preliminaries, such as collecting additional survival gear, must be performed before launching the raft.

The bottom line is that no matter the extent of the emergency, before any of the following actions are taken, think about the consequences of each action. Hasty and unplanned moves can exacerbate an already grave situation.

The following actions are essential in an abandon-ship situation, but the order in which they are taken will depend on the nature of the particular situation.

- Transmit a Mayday message; if possible continue transmitting until communication is established with rescue personnel. An essential part of the transmission—whether the transmission is acknowledged or not—must be the repeated position of the vessel as taken from the GPS and the number of people about to enter the water or the life raft. (See Chapter 8.)

- Ensure that all aboard are wearing personal flotation devices (PFDs) and are warmly dressed. Regardless of water and surface temperature, immersion even in seemingly warm water can induce hypothermia.

- Throw everything that might conceivably be of use into the life raft once it is inflated. "Everything" includes blankets, additional clothing, food, water, handheld portable radios, and GPS transmitters. If any knives or tools are taken on board, extreme care must be taken that sharp points are protected to avoid puncturing the raft.

- Have the crew attempt to enter the life raft directly from the mother vessel rather than going into the water before boarding the raft.

- Keep the life raft attached to the distressed vessel for as long as possible, unless the boat is on fire or about to sink. This may give you additional time to re-board the boat to collect more gear, and the larger boat represents a larger visible and radar target for search and rescue teams.

Once aboard the life raft, safely out of danger and having done everything appropriate to the situation to encourage rescue—utilizing pyrotechnics, deploying dye-markers, transmitting Maydays, etc.—it's time to wish for and expect rescue, but to act as if it might not be immediately forthcoming. Even if you *know* that rescue will be immediate, prepare for the long haul. See to the comfort and health of all aboard. Ensure that all are dressed warmly. Take stock of food and water supplies and whatever gear is present. Begin a practical rationing procedure. Determine position by whatever means possible (e.g., handheld GPS, or the logbook that you took off the boat) and begin a dead reckoning plot. Depending on how many are aboard, set up and maintain a watch schedule, with the person on watch directed to peer outside at regular intervals. Schedule activities such as eating and sleeping; a regimen, any regimen, will help stave off the lassitude and depression that can affect survival.

If you ever, by some lousy stroke of luck, find yourself there; keep the following in mind while hanging out in that life raft. The fact that you made it safely into the raft means the odds are overwhelmingly in your favor that you will survive and be rescued. Yes, there is nothing more depressing than peering out and seeing an endless expanse of cold gray or black ocean and you just *know* that you'll never be found; people have done regrettable things upon giving in to that depression. Don't. Just remember that you're looking at it from the perspective of a jellyfish and your horizon is minuscule. Your rescuers are searching from the perspective of an airplane or from the lofty bridge of a ship. They can see many, many miles and they will find you. Trust me; they found me—and that feeling of joy and relief will make it all worth it, well, almost. And after you get back ashore, begin looking for another boat—you know; the thing about getting back on the horse.

The Ditch Bag

MOST LONG-DISTANCE CRUISERS—those who routinely travel offshore for long periods of time—carry a ditch bag near at hand for instant retrieval and to toss into the life raft if disaster strikes. This bag contains the essentials that can make life aboard the raft bearable and sustainable. The die-hard cruiser might carry a dedicated ditch bag that is always stocked with gear that is stowed specifically for abandoning ship and never utilized for any other purpose. It is only opened to update degradable items like water and rations.

For most of us, such a ditch bag is just not practical. We don't go pleasure boating in expectation of disaster. However, it *is* practical to have aboard most of the items that should join you if it's ever necessary to abandon ship. Following is a list of items that I believe should be readily available. You should know where every item is on the boat. It is a good idea to make a list of the items and their locations and then post that list near the helm so nothing is forgotten. Some of these items may be included in the kit provided by the raft manufacturer, but certainly not all, so you should make your own kit, adding, eliminating, or substituting items as needed. As for the bag itself, a waterproof duffel or one made of sailcloth—available at most chandleries—will do just fine, and will fold away neatly in a minuscule space that everybody aboard should be aware of.

- Food and water: as many plastic gallon containers of water as it is possible to take aboard, high-energy food items such as energy bars and securely capped honey, and snack foods
- Medical items: sun-block, sunburn cream, seasickness remedies, over-the-counter pain and prescription medication in tightly sealed containers, petroleum jelly (i.e., Vaseline), toilet tissue (sealed in ziplock bags)
- Up-to-date flare kit, containing at least: one or two dye-marker packs; two or three handheld (orange) smoke flares; two or three red handheld flares; three or four red parachute flares
- Waterproof handheld VHF
- Waterproof manual 406 EPIRB (this must be registered in accordance with instructions included on the unit)
- One or two whistles and canister horns
- Signal mirror
- Two or three waterproof flashlights with spare batteries
- Hand-bearing compass
- Chemical lightsticks
- Digital waterproof watch
- Manual air pump for the life raft (Some rafts include this; if not, a pump designed for inflating water toys can be pressed into service.)
- Fishing gear: various safely packed fish-hooks and line that can be utilized as a drop line
- One or two knives: extreme care must be taken that the points are protected: folding knives preferred
- Ship's papers: logbook, registration/ documentation, charts of the area
- Personal papers of all aboard: passports, driver's licenses, cash
- Radar reflector (If not included with the raft, aluminum foil or an aluminum, iron, or stainless steel frying pan will do the job.)

Appendix
Books on Boating

Boat Buying

Getting Started in Powerboating. 2005. Bob Armstrong. International Marine: Camden, ME.
How to Choose Your First Powerboat. 1999. Chuck Gould. Sheridan House: Dobbs Ferry, NY.
Sorensen's Guide to Powerboats, 2nd Edition. 2007. Eric Sorensen. International Marine: Camden, ME.

Seamanship

Knots, Bends, and Hitches for Mariners. 2006. United States Power Squadrons. International Marine: Camden, ME.
Onboard Weather Handbook. 2008. Chris Tibbs. International Marine: Camden, ME.
Power Boaters Guide. 2006. Basil Mosenthal and Richard Mortimer. Adlard Coles: London.
Powerboat Handling Illustrated. 2007. Bob Sweet. International Marine: Camden, ME.
Powerboating Companion. 2007. Peter White. Wiley: New York.
RYA Powerboat Handbook. 2005. Paul Glatzel. Royal Yachting Association: Hampshire, UK.

Navigation

How to Read a Nautical Chart. 2002. Nigel Calder. International Marine: Camden, ME.
The Weekend Navigator. 2004. Bob Sweet. International Marine: Camden, ME.

Cruising

Coastal Cruising Under Power. 2006. Gene and Katie Hamilton. International Marine: Camden, ME.

The Compleat Cruiser. 1987. L. Frances Herreshoff. Sheridan House: Dobbs Ferry, NY.

Voyaging Under Power, 3rd Edition. 1994. Capt. Robert P. Beebe, Revised by James F. Leishman. International Marine: Camden, ME.

Index